BECAUSE
OF
HOPE

Because of Hope

Woman's Missionary Union
Published in conjunction with Iron Stream Media
100 Missionary Ridge
Birmingham, AL 35242
IronStreamMedia.com

Library of Congress Control Number: 2022909288

Cover design by For the Muse Designs

ISBN: 978-1-62591-377-7 (paperback)
WMU Product ID: W223105

1 2 3 4 5—26 25 24 23 22

BECAUSE
OF
HOPE

Reflections of Faith

WMU® God's mission.
Our passion.

Birmingham, Alabama

This book is dedicated to all fifty authors who wrote inspiring reflections. Thank you for encouraging us on our faith journey.

CONTENTS

CONTENTS

Acknowledgments

National WMU is grateful for Sandy Wisdom-Martin and Anne Wilson who had the privilege of compiling these incredible stories of faith.

To the Reader

Experience our extraordinary God through the journeys of fifty ordinary Christ followers. Through stories and devotional thoughts, you will immerse yourself with those who walked in obedience, faced unimaginable loss, persevered through hardship, overcame trials, witnessed incredible love and compassion, gained insight from God's Word, and found direction through prayer. We hope their reflections will leave you filled with hope in Christ.

This work contains accounts from people in all walks of life. With stories from missionaries, seminary professors, missions leaders, executives, and everyday men and women, you certainly will find encouragement and inspiration.

The words penned by each author will fuel your own faith. A Bible verse or passage accompanies every narrative. Combining Scripture with prayer and the power of individual stories will ignite your own passion to pursue God's mission. We believe you will echo the sincere belief of each author featured—hope is found in Christ alone.

If you have never personally experienced hope in Christ, we invite you to turn to the back of the book and read how to become a Christian. It is our sincere desire you receive Christ as your personal Lord and Savior.

Sandy Wisdom-Martin, executive director-treasurer, National Woman's Missionary Union

God Will Take Care of You

And why do you worry . . .? See how the flowers of the
field grow. They do not labor or spin.

—Matthew 6:28

I do not remember the first time I met Albert Peeks. As it was for many, it was for me—I had seen Albert walking up and down the streets just north of the First Baptist Church of Mineral Wells, Texas, where I was pastor. Albert was disheveled, somewhat confused, and disoriented at times. Sometimes he would be walking down the sidewalk, make an immediate turn, take off in another direction, and then change directions again.

One day he came by the church office and showed me his well-worn Bible. He told me he read it and tried to live by it. Then, he quickly turned and disappeared. It began a periodic conversation we had for several years.

From his oldest sister, Betty, I learned Albert's story. As a child, he was a voracious reader. He had a thirst for learning. He played the piano by ear. He also loved the outdoors and nature. The gospel had been passed down to him from his grandmother, who grew up in the home of a circuit-riding preacher. Her daughter, Albert's mother, assembled the six children together for daily Bible study and prayer.

Albert was the youngest. He had heard his mother pray in public and in private and observed her reading her Bible daily. Her faith was real. Albert made a commitment to Christ in early childhood at the Salesville Baptist Church, just north of Mineral Wells, and was baptized in Turkey Creek. He took his faith seriously—a faith from which he would never depart, even in the most challenging of life circumstances.

In Mineral Wells High School, Albert was a good student. On his eighteenth birthday, January 17, 1964, he joined the navy just four months shy of high school graduation. He left for the United States Navy Training Center in San Diego on February 5, 1964.

During a naval diving accident, Albert got tangled in a net and was unconscious when brought to the surface. He had suffered irrevocable brain damage due to oxygen deprivation. The navy honorably discharged Albert on March 10, 1964— having served thirty-five days—and placed him on a Greyhound bus with a name tag and his destination, "Mineral Wells, Texas," pinned to his shirt.

His parents and sister, Betty, were alerted to his arrival time. When Albert did not get off the bus, she asked the driver, "My brother is supposed to be on this bus."

He said, "There is a man on the back seat, but I've not been able to communicate with him."

Albert. He could not speak, nor recognize his sister or parents. His injury was not only physical, but emotional and psychological. His world had stopped. His parents took him home and tried to nurse him back to health.

For the next fifty-five years, Albert was in and out of veteran's hospitals and veteran-approved foster homes. With wanderlust, he traveled across this nation, lived in homeless shelters and on the streets. He was in and out of libraries with an insatiable hunger for knowledge, periodically returning to Mineral Wells. All the while, Albert was reading his Bible and attending worship in chapels and churches wherever he went. That's when I met Albert in the late 1990s. He was back in Mineral Wells and came to our church periodically.

On the eve of Christmas Eve, 2002, Betty called to say Albert was missing on a deadly cold night. She feared for his health.

With the help of Bobby Hart, a local justice of the peace, Albert was found. A deputy sheriff drove Albert to the Waco Veterans Administration Hospital. Hart was told, "Had you waited one more day, Albert would have died."

I visited Albert in that Waco hospital. Soon, he was well enough to be dismissed. He moved to Fort Worth. For the next five years, Albert disappeared. I feared he had died. He remained on our church prayer list.

On Mother's Day night, May 11, 2008, I got a phone call from Betty. Proudly, she told me that on Friday night, May 9, she and three family members attended the graduation ceremony at Tarrant County College in Fort Worth where Albert, at the age of sixty-two, had earned a diploma as a heating, air conditioning, and refrigeration repair technician. I was astounded and asked, "How did it happen?"

In Fort Worth, Albert met James McCoy, a "structural coach," who, in a men's home in East Fort Worth, helped men get "structure" back into their lives. Albert went to live there. He got his life under control. He took his medications regularly. He decided to go to college. At 5:30 each morning, Albert walked half a mile from "Jay's House," as it was called, to a bus stop. He caught the number 3 bus and then transferred to the number 4 bus. It took him to the south campus of Tarrant County College. He attended college three days a week. After class, Albert reversed his route to Jay's House. He did this for two years. To the other five men living in Jay's House, Albert was their hero. Albert gave them hope.

Two weeks later, I went looking for Albert in East Fort Worth. I found him and told him we were proud of him. He showed me his graduation photograph in cap and gown.

Along with fifteen graduates of Mineral Wells High School, I invited Albert to be recognized in our Sunday morning baccalaureate-style service at the church, but I wanted his entrance into the service to be a surprise. During the sermon conclusion, I told the congregation about Albert's college graduation. I challenged the graduates to never give up. Then,

I asked the rhetorical question, "I wonder what structural coach James McCoy would say about Albert if he were here?" From a microphone behind closed doors, McCoy responded, "Mark, we *are* here!"

Entering behind James McCoy, Albert, in cap and gown, strode to the pulpit as I beckoned him and McCoy to the platform. Never have I seen a church congregation rise to its feet in such a spontaneous, sustained, standing ovation with wave after wave of clapping. Five hundred church members clapping in wonder, surprise, joy, and encouragement.

Albert stood proud. The mixture of emotions evoked a lump in our throats, tears in our eyes, and a warm feeling in our hearts. The family of faith was encouraging Albert, the "least likely to succeed" in Mineral Wells.

We awarded Albert an honorary "Diploma of Perseverance," McCoy a "Diploma of Compassion," and Hart, who had saved Albert's life, another "Diploma of Compassion."

For the next eleven years, Albert persevered, and his sister Betty said, "He never gave up his Christian faith."

But life took its toll. On April 9, 2019, I spoke at Albert's funeral at the Salesville Baptist Church. The American flag draped his coffin. At the cemetery, a Navy Honor Guard provided a gun salute and a bugled "Taps." Fifty-five years of brain injury, but Albert persevered. God took care of him.

Once, after being beaten by some mean-spirited and prejudiced men, Betty asked him, "Aren't you afraid?"

Albert said, "God takes care of the flowers of the field. Don't you believe God takes care of us?"

Albert's life is a story of hope for all Christians.

Mark Bumpus retired in 2020 after forty-one years as a Texas Baptist pastor.

Beautiful Feet
Carrying Hope

How beautiful on the mountains are the feet of those
who bring good news, who proclaim peace, who bring
good tidings, who proclaim salvation, who say to Zion,
"Your God reigns!"

—Isaiah 52:7

The sight of feet is what I remember most. The landscape was dramatic, steep green hills rising from rice paddies. The cities were exotic, chaotic streets with three-wheeled auto rickshaws weaving around the occasional lazy cow and past ornate Hindu temples.

The food was aromatic and dangerously spicy. Weathered and dusty, dry and cracked, brown, bare feet. Above these feet were laps on which open Bibles rested, worn and well used. Within those sacred pages was found the verse that those feet brought to mind. Isaiah 52:7 begins, "How beautiful on the mountains are the feet of those who bring good news."

Those faithful feet bore the marks of many hard miles of bringing the good news of Jesus Christ to difficult places. They were the feet of the local missionaries, Indian men transformed by Christ and faithfully fulfilling the Great Commission by making disciples of the people of their tribes and villages.

I could see those feet from my vantage point standing at the podium. If I looked higher, I could see over the heads of the men taking notes and listening attentively, through the open back door of the building, to a small barnyard where several dark, broad-shouldered water buffalo were chewing hay.

I had been in India for a week as part of a mission team tasked with teaching and encouraging local missionaries at a conference. The local pastor we worked with had emailed us some suggested teaching topics for the conference. One of the topics he requested was the subject of persecution. India has seen persecution of Christians rise dramatically in the past several years alone as the result of an aggressively pro-Hindu government. I could understand why that subject would be relevant to the men we would teach.

The sudden increase in persecution for Christians meant that persecution was not just a distant possibility for these Indian Christians, it was a distinct probability. A year or so after my trip, the church building where the conference was held was vandalized, the interior trashed, and furniture broken and tossed around.

My shock when our friend sent us pictures of the damage sticks with me, even to this day. The church members simply cleaned up the mess and carried on. Around the same time as the vandalism, one of the pastors hosting the conference was falsely accused of abuse and jailed. Thankfully, God had a providentially placed policeman involved in the legal process and the accused pastor was cleared of charges, but not without a damaged reputation. He continues to joyfully serve the Lord, undeterred by false accusations and jail time. Another pastor, the one who hosted our team and helped us get around, spoke matter-of-factly of brothers and sisters in Christ around the country who had been imprisoned, beaten, and in some cases martyred for the cause of Christ.

In light of this reality, I was faced with a question. What could I possibly teach an Indian believer about persecution? Someone from the Bible Belt teaching these Indian brothers about persecution would be like one of them coming to my church in Alabama and giving a talk on college football. And yet that was the task to which I was assigned. What I didn't realize is that God had been preparing me to speak on the subject of persecution in advance, not from personal experience, but from the Bible.

Fortunately, God's Word has plenty to say on the subject of persecution. I had just been teaching through the first accounts of persecution against the church in the book of Acts. At the time I thought I was simply preparing to teach a men's Wednesday night Bible study at my church. I had no idea that God was preparing me to teach a room full of Indian missionaries and church planters on the other side of the world. Though I certainly couldn't speak from my own experience, I could share how God used persecution and the death of Stephen to spread and grow the early church in Acts chapter 7 and 8. The men expressed gratitude and were encouraged by God's Word.

At the end of several days of teaching, the conference ended. We did what one does at the end of every good church function. We ate. The women of the church had prepared a feast for us cooked outside in large pots. We sat around the grounds of the church property on plastic chairs eating together with pastors, missionaries, and their families. The afternoon light faded and the men began gathering their belongings.

As they filed out of the church, I saw those same well-worn Bibles tucked under their arms. I watched those same feet I had noticed while teaching. Those who had shoes slipped them back on. Some climbed onto small motorcycles to begin the journey back to their homes. Some simply walked off barefoot down the dusty roads, back to the task of spreading the gospel and making disciples of Jesus. How beautiful are the feet of those who bring good news.

Jon Jeffries serves as a denominational liaison and design editor for students at national WMU.

Courage to Cross
the Sidewalk

Have I not commanded you? Be strong and courageous.
Do not be afraid; do not be discouraged, for the LORD
your God will be with you wherever you go.

—Joshua 1:9

On a bright, sunny day in early October, I served as a Baptist Collegiate Ministry (BCM) Director and gathered with BCM students that morning for an outreach event in the common area in the middle of campus. Our goal was to begin spiritual conversations with students, while handing out toaster pastries as they walked to class. We never knew who we might encounter, so we needed to rely on the Holy Spirit for strength and boldness.

I arrived to set up our table and noticed two female students setting up a table across the sidewalk. I felt prompted to greet them.

After introducing myself, I asked, "What organization are you representing?"

One of them said, "P.R.O.T.E.C.T." I had heard of this group: Pagans Reaching Out To Educate Campus Together. Glancing at their literature, I saw information about the Salem witch trials, Wicca, and Halloween.

I said, "Nice to meet you," and quickly walked back to join the BCM students.

As we finished setting up our table and our toasted pastry outreach was underway, I felt the Lord saying, "Go back and talk to them. Tell them that I love them."

"But, Lord, they aren't interested. They're involved in witchcraft. I'm afraid," I thought.

"Don't be afraid. I will go with you. I will give you the words to say."

I swallowed hard and told the BCM students I was going back across the sidewalk, praying as I took those few steps. I explained we were a Christian group out on the quad today to give out free toasted pastries.

"Would you like one?" I asked. They declined. To further engage, I inquired about the information on the table. "Have you been to Salem?"

Both ladies became excited, jumping at this opportunity to share how they had not been to Salem, but wanted to go to see where people of their faith had been persecuted and had given their lives. They told me they were looking forward to Halloween when they could celebrate with other witches, drawing power from nature. The Lord allowed me to see how much these two young women were searching for peace and purpose. They were just looking in the wrong place.

"I understand your desire to visit Salem," I said. "I have visited Israel and saw the places where my Savior, Jesus, lived, ministered, died, and rose again. It was an amazing experience." I smiled. "I guess Halloween for you is like Christmas and Easter for Christians. Have you heard about Jesus? He loves you so much and gave His life for you."

They had heard about Jesus, but made it clear they didn't want to hear any more. I took that cue, excused myself, and went back to the BCM table.

Several minutes passed and another student approached the PROTECT table. He was dressed in black and wore a long purple cape with a pentagram embroidered on the back. With him seemed to come a dark, thick cloud of oppression. When he settled in at the table, I heard the Lord nudging, "Go back to them."

"Really? I can feel the evil in the air. I don't want to go talk to him. He looks scary."

"Don't be afraid. I will go with you."

Again, I swallowed hard and started across the sidewalk. The young man stood and sternly said, "Don't come over here!"

I stopped but managed to sheepishly say, "I just want to come over and talk to you."

"I know who you are, and I don't want you coming over here."

The Lord said, "Go. They need to hear about my love for them. Do not be afraid. I will lead the way."

In obedience, I took another step. The young man began to approach me, then stopped. He tried to come closer to me but could not. As I took another step, he backed up as if a barrier existed between us. I took another step and he took another step backward. My courage increased, and I kept moving forward.

Reaching the table, I said, "I know we worship different gods. I believe the god you serve hates the God I serve. But I want you to remember the God I serve loves you. He loves you so much that He sent His Son, Jesus, to die in your place, just like He died in my place. He rose from the dead to pave the way for us to have a relationship with Him. I sense you are searching and I believe Jesus is the answer. Please think about it," I said. "I hope you will choose to accept His love."

One of the young women stated she had never had a kind, nonconfrontational conversation with a Christian. She thanked me and said she would think about what I said.

Through this experience, the Lord proved that He will indeed give courage and be with me wherever He calls. I've learned to rely on the hope of Christ and trust Him as He led me to step out in courage over the years. I've had the opportunity to participate in mission trips overseas, see people come to Christ from other faiths, and to experience growth in my own faith.

In our lives, we may not be called to cross a major river like the Israelites. Sometimes we need courage to step across the sidewalk, or cross the street in front of our house, or go to the desk next to ours at work or walk across the cafeteria. A few steps can seem like a mile, but the Lord promises to go with us. Remember His words in Joshua 1:9: "Be strong and courageous. Do not be afraid; do not be discouraged, for the LORD your God will be with you wherever you go." So, trust the Lord and go with strength and courage, my friend.

Serena Butler retired in 2021 after serving twenty-nine years in various ministry roles across Illinois.

Taking Every Thought Captive

Finally, brothers and sisters, whatever is true, whatever
is noble, whatever is right, whatever is pure, whatever
is lovely, whatever is admirable—if anything is
excellent or praiseworthy—think about such things.

—Philippians 4:8

Controlling my thoughts. Oh, how I've struggled through
the years. Then God took me by the hand and taught
me the importance of taking every thought captive.
Honestly, I didn't believe I could do it. It seemed a hopeless task.
But I learned that in His strength, it was possible.

But it wasn't easy.

As a brand-new missionary, I basked in the glow of living
out my dream of ministering overseas in Russia. I knew many
faithful people were praying for me. Praying the prayer, "God
bless and protect the missionaries."

That glow shattered when two colleagues, a married couple,
were murdered. Brutally and cruelly. I'll never forget the face of
the messenger who came to tell us that these precious servants
had been found dead in their apartment.

My gut reaction was immediate. "God, if this is what you
sent me here for, I didn't sign up for this. I didn't come here to
die!" And instantly, shame shattered my heart. I was appalled at
my thoughts.

Goodness gracious, I had devoured missionary biographies as a youth. I'd forgotten that many of those stories spoke of hardship. Lottie Moon practically starved to death. William Carey's two wives died in India, with his first wife suffering a complete mental breakdown. Jim Elliot died at the hands of the people he went to reach. Somehow, I'd skimmed over the stories of suffering and focused on the excitement. The excitement of how people's lives were changed as they came into a relationship with Jesus.

The truth was I didn't want to learn about the struggles.

But God had another plan.

Within a few weeks, my family moved into the apartment where our colleagues were murdered. It's a long story, full of amazing lessons and miracles. Still, today, I want to focus on the lesson God taught me about taking every thought captive.

We moved into the furnished apartment with our two children. We walked the floors, sat on the furniture, and slept in the beds of our martyred colleagues. After we moved in, the local Russian police visited and said they couldn't protect us if we insisted on living there. But God gave our family an overwhelming peace about living in this apartment. We knew He put us in this home for a reason.

Most of the time, I didn't dwell on the murders.

Until nighttime.

Every night, I sat on my side of the bed and stared at the carpet under my feet—where the body of the murdered wife was discovered.

I'd lie down and horrific images would flood my mind. Different scenarios of how this missionary woman struggled and fought her attacker replayed over and over in my thoughts. In my imagination, I felt her pain. Sleep evaded me. Sometimes I could barely breathe. Silent tears streamed down my face as I tried not to disturb my husband's sleep.

During this same period, my nine-year-old daughter also struggled with her own set of fears. Learning a new language and culture, riding public transportation, missing America, all those things had already impacted my daughter's life. Our older son also had his share of struggles but was not as fearful as our younger daughter.

And now we lived in an apartment where murders occurred. I still flinch when I recall my daughter's anxious question: "When will they come to shoot us?"

We had not shared all the details surrounding the murders, and she didn't know someone had been shot. Agonized thoughts swirled around in my head, and I wondered if my children's lives would be forever scarred by this experience.

As I searched for a way to help my daughter and myself, God brought Philippians 4:8 to my mind.

"Finally, brothers and sisters, whatever is true, whatever is noble, whatever is right, whatever is pure, whatever is lovely, whatever is admirable—if anything is excellent or praiseworthy— think about such things."

I printed the verse out for my daughter. I suggested we work together to conquer our fears by following the instructions in Philippians 4:8. Whenever frightening thoughts filled our minds, we would turn our focus to truth, the truth of God's Word, and to lovely, excellent, and praiseworthy things. Most importantly, we turned our hearts over to Jesus, our light in a dark world, our Living Hope, the One who walks beside us.

Finally, I again slept peacefully. Scenes of violence no longer occupied my thoughts and dreams. With God's help, I controlled my thoughts and dwelt on heavenly things.

One morning a couple of weeks later, my daughter ran to me and excitedly said she'd had a dream about our martyred colleagues. She'd dreamt that they were in heaven, looking down at our family, and they were happy we were living in their apartment. My heart rejoiced to see God's Word calming my daughter's fears.

Several months later, while stripping off wallpaper in my son's bedroom, I noticed tiny pink splatters on the wallpaper. I wondered what my son had spilled in his room. Then I realized, it was faded blood splatters of the murdered husband.

I'd heard the statement that contentment comes from a shift in attitude, not a change of circumstances. Oh, how I ached to change this circumstance. Yes, I would have preferred to live in a lovely, new apartment without bloodstains. But instead, God allowed me to walk where martyrs had walked. He used a painful circumstance to teach me about contentment, finding hope, and taking my thoughts captive.

Oh, the blessings God sent our way.

Out of that blood-stained apartment, many students came to know a Savior who shed His blood for their salvation. Our work with students resulted in a thriving church that recently celebrated its twenty-fifth anniversary.

And I learned the truth of Philippians 4:13: "I can do all things through Christ who strengthens me" (NKJV).

Even taking every thought captive.

Robin Covington served with the IMB for twenty-two years and currently works as the executive ministry assistant at Rabbit Creek Church, in Anchorage, Alaska. Connect with Robin at robinleecovington.com.

Spirit Speak

I have much more to say to you, more than you can now bear. But when he, the Spirit of truth, comes, he will guide you into all the truth. He will not speak on his own; he will speak only what he hears, and he will tell you what is yet to come. —John 16:12–13

One of my favorite topics to talk about is awakenings. I love the thought of the Kingdom of God moving widespread, kind of like an epidemic, through a large area. I love the unnumbered stories of revivals throughout the centuries. The idea of God using a small piece of His Church to be the mouthpiece for a large group of lost people to hear fascinates me. Two experiences that have impacted me the most occurred in foreign countries.

I was part of the leadership for my very first international mission trip. The destination was deep in the country of Mexico. My assignment was to lead one third of our group on daily prayer walks throughout the villages surrounding our target area. A large group from the church I pastored was present, and it was the first time for most of them to be out of the country. I was scared out of my wits.

One day, toward the end of the day, we were walking back to our host village. We had a long evening ahead of us filled with a meal, an extensive worship service, and the drive back to our hotel. We had quite a distance to walk before we even got to the village, and I saw a house.

One person was sitting on the front steps of the house. I quietly prayed, "Lord, I'm exhausted. We've shared the gospel with so many today. Do we really need to stop at this last house?" I made a deal with the Lord. I would speak to the man. Just a simple greeting. If he acknowledged us, we would step through the gate, into the yard, and ask a few questions. If he said nothing, we would keep walking.

Quickly, quietly, and without much eye contact, I uttered, "Hello!"

The man stood and asked us to join him in his yard. I rolled my eyes. He asked us who we were and why we were walking the streets in his village. We briefly told him we were a part of a church that worshipped Jesus and were in his village to tell people how God created them for a relationship with Him. He stopped us at that last sentence and asked us to wait.

He went in the house and retrieved seventeen people he said needed to hear what we had to say. Seventeen people? This large family more than filled the front porch and lawn of that small house, eagerly listening to what must have been our fiftieth gospel conversation of the day. Many of them prayed to receive Christ that day and we left extremely excited and encouraged.

I learned an important lesson on that gravel road in Mexico. Awakenings are God's work, not ours. We are hard-pressed to anticipate or plan our way into them. Our best efforts come with weak knees and tired hearts. When we offer a simple yes the sky is the limit with what God will do.

The second story took place in Peru. As our team met to pray over our fifteenth trip to this region, the only direction we had from the Lord was to go to a specific town. That was it. Just "go."

On that trip we had one hundred solar-powered mp3 players loaded with the first ten stories of Creation to Christ and the Gospel of Mark. The first day we took a mountain taxi to the village and before we ever set foot inside the town of fifteen hundred people, we met a man eager to hear the gospel. That first morning we barely made it one hundred yards down the first street. I had never been in a place where people were so hungry to hear from the Lord. At lunch, we met the foreman of a large construction company. They had contracted to build the local secondary school. They asked us to speak to their men that evening.

We gathered in the small basement that night not knowing what to expect. These were hard construction workers. I asked our biggest guy to share the story of Moses. He was a construction worker and I prayed God would use him to speak their language. When he finished, I preached for about an hour to a rapt audience. We didn't often give invitations in Peru because of the hospitality culture. People will tell you what they think you want to hear. It is their way of encouraging you and showing love.

That night, however, I felt the Spirit saying, "Ask them."

I said, "We've talked tonight about what it means to walk with Jesus. This is not a one-time decision. This is a lifestyle He is asking you to adopt. Does anyone in this room want to walk with Jesus?"

One man at the end of the table raised his hand and said, "In total!"

I didn't understand.

He said, "We all do."

I asked the question again. "We are not just talking about heaven. We are talking about God creating you for a relationship with Him now. Jesus makes that possible. Do you want to lay down your life so Jesus can live through you? It's painful, hard work." I was not the most encouraging preacher, but we were not there for numbers. Our prayer was that God would raise up disciples in those mountains.

Again, the group responded, "We all do!"

That night an entire construction company of about thirty men responded to God's invitation to join Him in His work around them. The mountains began to shift as did my heart. I learned the work of awakenings is surprising and unpredictable. Years of hard labor in the field can produce little fruit and one night of yielding to God's will can change a region. The work of awakenings is done primarily by the Spirit. Our plans, dreams, hopes, and desires are nothing if not filled with and moved by Him. My only job is to move with Him.

Daniel Bramlett is pastor of First Baptist Church Hope, Arkansas.

The Impossible Dream

Jesus looked at them and said, "With man this is impossible, but with God all things are possible."

—Matthew 19:26

In rapid succession, soldiers dashed into the house. They did not knock on the door or ask for permission. The soldiers marched into the dining room where the family of four ate their evening meal.

The leader of the group addressed the father. "I've heard you were talking about the government, and you did not approve of the party's policies. I have heard you bought an extra pound of meat this month. I've heard . . . I've heard . . . I've heard."

They did not give facts or evidence. The soldier simply uttered, "I've heard . . ."

In a communist country like Cuba there is no *innocent until proven guilty*. There are no search warrants. There is no freedom of speech and no trial by your peers, as in the United States.

The father was quickly taken away, and his wife and two daughters were left behind not knowing what would happen next. The following day, miraculously, the father was released. He came home to inform his family their house had been seized by the government, and they would have to leave immediately. Additionally, his business had also been taken over by the government and their bank accounts had been frozen.

The family was frightened but not shaken. Why? Because the mom knew and believed God was in control of this situation, and God had a perfect plan for her family.

After several months of living with relatives, the couple discussed the possibilities of starting over in the United States. This began the long and difficult process of obtaining visas and documents to travel to the US.

In the fall of 1960, the father traveled alone to the United States so he could look for employment and a place for his family to live. He soon moved in with a friend in a one-bedroom efficiency apartment and immediately started working as a dishwasher in a local restaurant. The once-successful businessman now walked each day to a restaurant and worked for sixteen hours a day washing dishes.

The mom and daughters stayed behind in their homeland because of difficulties with their visas, but finally, they were cleared and scheduled to travel to the United States at the end of January 1961. However, on January 3, the mom received a call from the US informing her that she and her daughters needed to catch a flight that night as Cuba and the US were about to break diplomatic relations. As a result, all flights would stop.

She packed a small suitcase, and a friend graciously gave her a five-dollar bill. She and her daughters promptly headed to the airport. At the airport, a gate attendant informed her the flight was overbooked by thirteen people.

The mom, full of faith and determination, told the attendant, "Put our names on the waiting list."

He said, "Lady, you are crazy!"

They sat. They waited. They prayed. The mom prayed to her Savior that if it was His will that they travel to the United States that night, He would do the impossible and reserve the last three seats for her family. Boarding for the flight began.

The words "Lady, you are crazy" rang loud in my mind.

My mom was not crazy, though. She was a woman of faith. She demonstrated unshakeable faith in her Savior. My mom walked in a close relationship with God. She placed her eyes upon Jesus even in the most impossible of situations. She was courageous and faithful. She stood firm and was not shaken.

In Mathew 19:26, we read, "With man this is impossible, but with God all things are possible." As a young girl, in that moment, I witnessed God taking the impossible and making it possible. Yes, this painful, frightening, and unforgettable experience forever changed me. The Lord Jesus Christ reserved the last three seats for my family. In that impossible moment, a new journey of hope and possibility began.

Our story of faith continued as my family reunited in Orlando, Florida. We did not speak English. We did not have money, but my mom knew Who controlled our future. For the next couple of weeks, I thought America was wonderful. I could sleep late, did not have to go to school, or do homework. My vacation came to an end when Mom announced she was going to enroll us in school.

The next day, I walked alone into my third-grade classroom. I was scared, and my teacher was not nice or kind. I did not understand her words, but I could feel her heart. I remember when she talked with me, she spoke very loudly. I kept thinking, "I can hear you. I am not hard of hearing. I just do not understand your words."

My difficult days in this classroom impacted my life forever. The Lord placed me in this specific classroom because He knew that, one day, I would work for Orange County Public Schools as senior administrator, responsible for the implementation of education for second-language learners. Again, God was in complete control. In a difficult, horrific, and seemingly impossible situation, God was at work. He was preparing me for a very specific task, and He alone was making it possible.

The next step for our family was to find a church. We walked to a church near our home. My mom showed the usher her Bible, *God's Holy Word*, because she could not yet speak English. This man knew and understood we were there to worship the God of all people.

The God who "so loved the world, that he gave his only begotten Son, that whosoever believeth in him should not perish, but have everlasting life." We were welcomed and loved.

Together, we glorified the God who makes all things possible. My entire life has been a triumphant journey of hope in spite of difficult circumstances.

Irma Moss is a former WMU president for Florida Women's Missions and Ministries.

Delivered from Drugs

Do you not know that your bodies are temples of the
Holy Spirit, who is in you, whom you have received
from God? You are not your own; you were bought at a
price. Therefore honor God with your bodies.

—1 Corinthians 6:19–20

Tylenol, Advil, and prayer would have to suffice. Newly
delivered from drug addiction, Kim Gustin couldn't risk
taking narcotic painkillers while recovering at home after
an appendectomy.

Her husband Gary was in the same fix as he struggled with
heptitis C.

Their doctor, a praying Christian, unbeknownst to them
understood.

"We told him that we were recovering addicts and
that we wanted to be held accountable," Gary said. "A lot of
people when they get into recovery, they want to start using
prescription drugs because it's legal. We were telling him we
don't want pain medicines and stuff like that. And he was very
kind and gracious."

Kim used prescribed narcotic drugs while in the hospital as
the anesthesia wore off from her operation but went home to
continue recovering with only over-the-counter pain killers and
praying often.

Kim and Gary had found hope on New Year's Day 2017
when they walked into Colt Baptist Church in small-town Colt,
Arkansas, in tattered clothes. They were living in a decaying

trailer about a half mile from the church, siphoning electricity from neighbors and taking five-gallon jugs of water from the outside hydrant at a business down the road. They had run out of food.

"We stunk," Gary said. "We were just completely lost."

He and Kim accepted Jesus that night. The two sensed an instantaneous delivery from decades of drug and alcohol addiction and everything that lifestyle can entail, including theft, lies, several jail stints, alienation from family and friends, and running from a lifestyle they loathed but couldn't shake. They joined Colt Baptist Church by baptism and were married on February 6, 2017.

Today, the two lead ministry outreach in the same town of about 350 people, a town so small it seemed everyone knew Kim and Gary were drug addicts. They now rent a small home, have a car, and are recovering from the physical side effects of the drugs they abused.

They founded a drive-through prayer ministry, praying for drivers who stopped briefly along the roadside. Gary began ministering at an area jail. Twice a month in 2021, they began sharing their testimonies with recovering addicts during a new Bible study at a residential drug treatment facility whose program is not faith-based, thereby helping take the gospel into new territory.

The Gustins see a need for Christianity in such treatment programs as Alcoholics Anonymous and Narcotics Anonymous that reference a "higher power" instead of the one true God.

"We're definitely wanting to change that thinking, to take the higher power and take it directly to Jesus," Kim said, "and show them that the higher power is God. That's it."

The couple's relationship with God has changed the way they treat their own bodies and hearts.

"For me, my body is a temple because God is indwelling," Kim said, "and He will indwell in me if I keep it as a temple He is wanting to be in. And if I put drugs and alcohol in my body, He surely is not going to be there with me, and I need to keep it a place where He would want to indwell in me."

"Abiders are diers," is the way she describes it. "Abiding in Him means I have to die to myself."

Gary shares his heart.

"When the Holy Spirit enters you, (He) enters through the mind and the heart. . . . A lot of people miss God by eighteen inches from their head to the heart. So I believe the heart is the temple," Gary said. "I look at God as my Father, and I don't want to disrespect Him. I don't want to let Him down, so I try to do my best to honor and glorify Him."

Gary experienced a breakthrough in his years-long struggle with hepatitis C the same day he began a new full-time job making copper tubing at a local factory.

"I had contracted it in prison, sharing needles with many other people there," Gary said. "At one point in time . . . they had checked my liver and everything else, and there was all kinds of scarring on my liver, and this is before I started the treatment."

Gary went through an unsuccessful course of Harvoni, a daily pill used to treat hepatitis C, and was among the 3 percent of patients the drug doesn't cure. Gary tells the experience of attending a revival at a local church when the revivalist—otherwise a stranger to him—called him up for prayer, with others laying hands on him. He returned to the doctor for another hepatitis C treatment, this time a pill called Vosevi.

"I went through the Vosevi treatment and was cured. It's only by the grace of God that I was," Gary said. "I give Him all the glory for it. So now I'm trying to take the gift that God has given me of life and trying to share it with other people."

Gary expresses a joy he doesn't "know how to put into words. God gave me back my life again. Awe-inspiring. I was just so thankful. I have no words that are good enough to say what He's done for me. I was just so honored that He would cure me. That He would give me a job and I can now help support my family. That I can do the things I couldn't do before. Gratitude. Just pure gratitude."

Kim and Gary are on track to celebrate five years of sobriety, marking their deliverance that occurred at Colt Baptist Church.

"The smell of our church is just like the smell of fresh-baked cookies," Kim said. "It's just that smell of walking into Grandma's house, coming home. I don't know how to describe it, except it's just like that. Every time we're in that church it's like coming home, every day."

Diana Chandler is a senior writer for Baptist Press in Nashville, Tennessee.

Joy Comes in the Morning

For his anger lasts only a moment, but his favor lasts a lifetime; weeping may stay for the night, but rejoicing comes in the morning.

—Psalm 30:5

I've been married twice. The first time, I had the opportunity to meet, court, and eventually marry a sweet and beautiful, young Christian girl named Teresa. We met and spoke our first words while attending college, though I had noticed her a number of years earlier. We went to the same elementary, middle, and high school, but we definitely did not run in the same circles. She was smart, musically gifted, and above all, one of the prettiest girls in the school. I, on the other hand, was what we called in the mountains a "simple country boy."

I met Teresa during my second year of college and from the beginning, she saw something in me that no one else had ever seen: potential. Four years later, we were married, and I was on my way to much learning and cultural refinement. Teresa encouraged me to grow and envision the man I could be. Between going with me to seminary, partnering in pastoring churches, having babies, and keeping home and heart together, she was the center of my existence. She passed from my life after thirty-one years of marriage when cancer robbed me of the one person I thought would always be there and would always see the best in me.

Darkness and loneliness are two of the characteristics of the night. When I entered the deep valley known as widowhood after being a happily married man, the darkness began to close in and my soul began to shrivel within me. Looking back now, I find myself marveling at the many times God intervened to keep me safe, sane, and sound. There were a few times when the reality of life beckoned more than the light of heaven and I thought longingly of reaching for permanent relief. The one barrier to those thoughts was a grandson whom I would leave behind wondering why his poppy chose to leave him in that way and not face with courage the overwhelming darkness.

One morning while I sat at my kitchen table, I wept. With tears falling on the pages of my Bible, I cried out to Jesus. "You promised You would not leave me. Why do I feel so alone?"

In the inexorable silence that followed came a quiet voice within my heart. Jesus spoke, "I promised to never leave you. My presence is not found in your feelings but guaranteed by My promise. I'll never leave you."

I decided I would remain a single man who carried with him the constant pain of separation and loss. Surprisingly, after a couple of very dark years, God intervened in my life with the introduction of another beautiful woman named Pennie. Now, Pennie had also enjoyed a wonderful marriage of thirty-two years to a godly man named Bob. They met while very young, married young, and had their three daughters at a young age. They were looking forward to enjoying life together when cancer became their enemy as well. After a valiant fight of more than two years, Bob left behind a grieving widow and a family that struggled to fill an unfillable emptiness.

It was at this point in my life that God began to speak. A church member came to my office one day and shared that he knew someone I needed to meet and her name was Pennie. I immediately informed him that I was not finished with my grieving, and I wasn't interested in meeting anyone else. I was adamant, but he was insistent and did not give up.

That church member reached out to Pennie and shared my pain with her. She, too, was not looking for another relationship and easily deflected his encouragement until he happened to mention, "Joe just needs a friend."

With those words, God started the journey of our love and healing. Under God's leadership, Pennie began praying for me and eventually reached out with a carefully written email. I responded and things just sort of went from there. We emailed back and forth for some time, but I found myself struggling to adjust to a friendship that had neither a face nor a voice.

With great planning, I would call Pennie and tell her whatever this was between us was not working and that I thought we should stop emailing each other. My thinking was that our final conversation would not continue more than ten minutes. With great trepidation, I phoned her and launched into my monologue about how this wasn't working. Somewhere along the line, I got off track and about an hour and a half later, I decided I wanted to talk to this woman some more.

We started to phone each other every few nights and talk for a couple of hours each time. Before long, I found myself needing to meet the owner of this lovely voice, spirited attitude, and Christlike personality. We decided to meet at the local barbeque joint in case one of us didn't look like we sounded.

She stopped at the door. I watched her carefully adjust her clothing before entering. I was smitten. I did not know it at the time, but God had answered my cry from the darkness. We love to tell our story. It took me one whole year from the very beginning to kiss her, another nineteen days before I asked for her hand in marriage, and finally, another sixteen days to make her my wife. That's been almost five years ago now and I must admit, God is good. Weeping may join you in the darkness but "Praise God!" rejoicing comes in the morning.

Joe Wright is the executive director of Bivocational and Small Church Leadership Network with Pennie working in the ministry as well.

In the Waiting

Be still before the Lord and wait patiently for him; do
not fret when people succeed in their ways, when they
carry out their wicked schemes.

—Psalm 37:7

How does one know the Lord has spoken? Was it Him or a dream? Did the words come from heaven or from our own being? Are we called in His will, or do we exercise our will to validate a call? Do others seem to have His blessings when we languish in fear or self-pity?

Learning about God's plan and His will in my life has never come easy and often with unwelcome drama. Stepping out in both fear and faith characterized the preparations for my first international mission trip. The Lord had made it clear to me that I would be unable to lead my church to be a light to the nations if I were unwilling to go to the nations. So, after a two-year struggle with God, I surrendered, signed up, and set out to follow the Lord to the country of Haiti. Just a few days into my first missions experience, our truck was held at gunpoint by an armed gang. Little had I known that morning that I was traveling into the epicenter of a coup that days later would be featured on CNN and weeks later would lead to the ousting of the current dictator.

Since that initial experience, I have led many mission trips and have catalyzed hundreds more. Not all short-term mission experiences make the news, but all are important to

God's plan. You should be seeking the Lord regarding your participation in missions.

Before heading to Haiti on that initial trip, my wife said she would be praying for me each day at 11:15 a.m. She had a break between projects at that time of the day and found it easy to spend those moments with the Lord. Desperately praying for God's help in Gonaïves that morning, I was assured of His presence as I looked down at my watch and noted it was 11:15 a.m.

During one of our trips in a military vehicle, the Haitian pastor who was leading our group descended from the cab to confront a gang leader. After introducing himself to the leader, the pastor was surprised that he was known by this man. A short time later, he explained to us still somewhat frightened mission team members that two years before this encounter, the gang leader had shown up at the pastor's house hungry and needing a place to stay.

The pastor took him into his home and fed him. Sharing food in this poor country is a high value. The hungry and homeless man had been blessed and was ready, even eager, to return the blessing. The angry crowd stepped back at the leader's bold direction, and we were allowed to pass on to our destination. Yes, the Lord hears a spouse's prayers at 11:15 a.m., and we know that He is there at any time of need.

David challenged us in Psalm 37:7 to "be still before the Lord and wait patiently for him." No matter what schemes are currently playing out around you—gangs, guns, or out-of-control teenagers—God offers the power to be still and to wait patiently. You can be still because God is in control. You can be patient because you can place your hope in Him. He is faithful.

David also states in the passage that we are not to fret. Fretting is the enemy of faith. We fret because we feel it is not going to work out, we feel God may not be in control, or we feel we need to take back control.

As a young man, our interim pastor Phil Hunter once said, "Friend, if you are in control, then you are out of control." Not being in control is an uncomfortable place to be unless you have allowed the One who is in control of the universe to be in complete control of your life. This type of dependence leads to stillness and patience.

I wonder if the psalmist was familiar with this verse from Lamentations 3:25–26 when he wrote today's passage? "The LORD is good to those whose hope is in him, to the one who seeks him; it is good to wait quietly for the salvation of the LORD."

Notice the writer shares it is good to wait quietly. It is not easy. It is good. Allow me to confess. I would rather drive by a restaurant with a line than wait for a table. I am attracted to call-ahead seating, fast passes, and express lanes.

I envy the travelers who get the pre-check status from the TSA while the masses wait in the long airport security lines. But the one who offered the testimony, "It was worth the wait," makes it clear that the blessings at the end far exceed our pain and efforts in the struggle to get there. It is good to wait quietly for the salvation of the Lord.

If you are writhing with this challenge, you are not alone. I preach to my own fear as I seek to inspire your faith. To borrow a common phrase these days, "God's got this." You can trust Him!

As we pulled out of that besieged and deadly Haitian town, I thought about the two years I was fighting the Lord about being faithful to follow Him on a mission trip. I thought that while I was hesitant to be faithful, God, in His providence, was being faithful to me by providing for my protection from the kindness of a local pastor. I left my fear of missions that morning in Gonaïves. My Gonaïves moment taught me I do not need to be afraid when God is in control. Just be still and patiently wait.

Mark Emerson is an associate executive director of Illinois Baptist State Convention.

Holy, Wholly, Holey

We have much to say about this, but it is hard to
make it clear to you because you no longer try to
understand. In fact, though by this time you ought
to be teachers, you need someone to teach you
the elementary truths of God's word all over again.
You need milk, not solid food! Anyone who lives on
milk, being still an infant, is not acquainted with the
teaching about righteousness. But solid food is for the
mature, who by constant use have trained themselves
to distinguish good from evil.

—Hebrews 5:11–14

The night of the musical, during a short snack break, I saw
my son, Jack, who'd been practicing all afternoon with the
youth choir. "Hey," he said, looking at my new blue velvet
skirt, "lookin' good!"

"Thanks," I said, surprised. "What do you want?" No fourteen-
year-old son gives his mother a compliment without an ulterior
motive. "I do need a favor, Mom. I left my good shoes at home.
These old tennis shoes don't match my suit . . . gotta get those
shoes!" I'd already eaten, so I left quickly to pick up the shoes (a
few blocks away) while he enjoyed the youth snacks.

Driving home, I practiced the women's trio alto part for
"Holy, Holy, Holy." I sang it until I was satisfied my pitch was
perfect. Looking into the car mirror, I practiced my holiest facial

Edna Ellison, *Deeper Still: A Woman's Study to a Closer Walk with God* (Birmingham: New Hope, 2006).

expressions. Then I looked down at the blue skirt. "You even look holy," I said to myself, stroking the velvet fabric, which I had cut and sewn myself. I was even holier because my hands had created the outfit. I was really going to be "lookin' good" singing a holy song, looking super holy in that velvet skirt!

It was dark by the time I got home. I ran through the darkened carport toward the kitchen door. Suddenly I stumbled over Jack's dirt bike, propped up on a cement block for repair. Falling over the motorcycle, I made a three-point landing with my knees on the block and my chin on the bottom step at the back door. The rough brick steps scratched my chin. I ran quickly inside, grabbed Jack's shoes, checked my watch, and then looked in the mirror. My chin was bleeding! I pressed a clean wet washcloth against it, knowing the bleeding would stop in a few minutes. At the last minute, I grabbed a bottle of foundation makeup to cover the spot and ran out the door.

On the way to the church the bleeding stopped. I relaxed and then noticed my skirt—right in the middle of the front was an L-shaped tear about two inches in each direction. I arrived at the church disheveled and out of breath. "What will I do?" I said to the other women in the trio, after I'd given the shoes to Jack. They grabbed the makeup and dabbed it over the red scratch on my chin. Then they turned the skirt back to front so that the tear would not be noticeable—at least not to anybody in the congregation. The choir was all smiles when I stepped out to the microphones as my legs showed through the velvet skirt. After the trio's song, I backed up stiffly without turning and sat down on the second row in the choir loft. Afterward, one of the men grinning in the choir said, "Edna, as you sang 'Holy, Holy, Holy,' you were wholly holey!"

Since then, I realized his remark is true: most of us sing about holiness, but we have holes in our souls. You might say we are wholly holey—we say proper words and hold our mouths just right in church to sound and look holy—but the truth is we will never be completely holy until we get to heaven. Our only holiness comes from accepting Christ. No good works can ever bring us holiness, but as He, the Most Holy One, lives inside our spirits, we become more like Him.

The Bible compares God's holy people—that is, those *sanctified*, or *made holy* through Him—with the world: the holy ones are mature; the unholy ones are immature (amateurs of the faith), or babes, in Christ. As a Christian, *holy* describes you. *Holy* is who we are as the people of God. Inside us, because we are God's people, wells up a yearning to become *who we are*! Sometimes we feel awkward, embarrassed, or incomplete if we accepted Christ but have never grown in our spiritual maturity and accepted His holiness set before us.

At times, we fail to see His holiness even when it is offered. It's a mysterious thing hidden in the darkness. I stumbled over Jack's motorcycle in the dark. However, the darkness began in my car, even before I got to the house. It began with my pride, as I looked in the mirror, practiced "looking holy," listened to the sound of my own voice mouthing "Holy, Holy, Holy," and took pride in *my* handmade skirt. I knew I was "lookin' good"! I hadn't focused on singing praise to God. I concentrated on my perfect sound, my perfect look, my perfect family—*my* everything. I had missed the mark of holiness completely. I stumbled and fell spiritually as well as physically that night.

Do you remember a time when your perfect façade was shot with holes? Pray about your spiritual maturing, asking for personal holiness. Do not become entangled in external rituals as a means to spiritual maturity. Hope is found in Christ alone. Spiritual maturity is a by-product of the working of the Holy Spirit of Christ in your life and your willingness to submit to His spiritual discipline.

Edna Ellison is a well-known author and speaker from Spartanburg, South Carolina.

Promises for Entering New Seasons

There is a time for everything, and a season for every
activity under the heavens.

—Ecclesiastes 3:1

As I write this, the green foliage on the trees is on the cusp
of turning fiery reds, blazing oranges, and brilliant golds.
Where there used to be sweltering heat, there's now a
subtle and welcome crispness in the air.

But as we're transitioning out of one season into another,
this shift in climate is only a reminder that change is inevitable.
The trees will give way to winter. But these bare branches will
offer the promise of new growth in a season to come.

Just like God has coded different seasons into the patterns
of nature, He has also written different seasons into the scripts
of our lives. As sure as we'll see winter, spring, summer, and fall,
we'll undergo change. I've seen this played out over and over in
my life, particularly in ministry.

When I was called to pastor my first church, I experienced a
bit of holy whiplash. I was doing my thing as a college minister.
When the senior pastor felt the pull to retirement, the leaders
of the church approached him without my knowledge saying,
"What about this rookie we have in the ranks? Could he do it?"

I'll never forget the night they called at 9:00 p.m. My wife,
Lynley, and I were at home with our first two babies. The
chairman of the deacons called and asked if I would come to

the church immediately. I told Lynley I thought I was about to get fired.

Out of a sense of urgency, I drove to the church still wearing the T-shirt and jeans I donned at home that evening. When I walked into the room, I saw a large semicircle of forty chairs facing a single empty chair.

I was asked to sit in that chair. It felt as though I was sitting before the Jewish Sanhedrin, or in this case, the Baptist Supreme Court. The chairman of the board shared that the leaders had elected to call me as the next pastor of the church.

I felt unqualified, but God called me. That night the deacons laid hands on me and prayed, and Lynley and I knew without a shadow of a doubt that this was the beginning of a new season.

Years later, through a series of events and heart change, the Lord called me and my family to a new assignment in Denver, Colorado. Our mission was to plant a church in this place where very few had the hope of Jesus woven into the fabric of their lives. This was an amazing journey. We saw our church plant through several seasons—from meeting in our basement to meeting at a school to buying and remodeling a building.

We made dear friends in our neighborhood and were energized by forming relationships with people whose worldview differed from ours. Things were happening. Lives were being changed.

Then just as abruptly as when God called me into my first pastorate, this time He called me and my family to pick up and move back East. But not to pastor a church. This time, I was being called out of my comfort zone to lead Lifeway Christian Resources.

As I look back on these changes and others in my life and ministry, each new season had in common three things. I believe they will prove true as God turns a new leaf in your life.

1. You likely have no idea what the next season entails.

Forrest Gump said, "Life was like a box of chocolates. You never know what you're gonna get." Expect the unexpected. I never dreamed I would be called to lead Lifeway I thought I'd be in Denver for the rest of my life planting churches there.

None of us knows what God has planned. For those of you planners reading this, take heed: Planning is a good thing, but throughout Scripture, we are warned about placing too much confidence in our calendar.

It's right to set some goals and to create our lists of next actions. Planning prevents the waste of time. But be prepared for God to bring you into a new season without notice.

2. You will likely feel ill-equipped for a new season.

Over and over in Scripture, when God moves people into a new season, those individuals often feel like fish out of water. There is a gap between their skill set and the assignment. That gap is where faith is allowed to grow.

God wants to show through insurmountable situations that He is able to fill in the gaps for us—if we will let Him. God likes to use people with gaps because those gaps are spaces where spiritual growth spikes like buds on a tree in spring.

3. You will experience a filling of the Holy Spirit to guide and sustain you through new seasons.

The most important thing you'll need to enter into a new season is the hand of God on your life. Jesus said, "Apart from me you can do nothing" (John 15:5).

Here's the reward of having a willing heart to step out of your comfort zone and into a new season: As you walk into a new season, you experience the power of the Holy Spirit. The reason many of us don't experience this power is because we don't leave what's easy. We've gotten too comfortable in our current season.

The bottom line is this: Whether you're stepping into a new season (joyfully or reluctantly) or you're in a holding pattern of a current season, the hope we have in Christ sustains us through it all.

Ben Mandrell is the president and chief executive officer of Lifeway Christian Resources.

Hope in a Dying Moment

For to me, to live is Christ and to die is gain.

—Philippians 1:21

My friend Doris was dying. More than a friend, she was a surrogate grandmother for our children and my word game nemesis. Her son called, told me the end was near, and asked me to come if I could. I cleared my schedule, jumped on a plane, and got to her hospital room later that night.

When I arrived, Doris was sleeping. Her son and I spent the next few hours sitting through the night in her room, sharing stories, and reminiscing about the remarkable life this remarkable woman had lived. We spoke about her caring spirit, her servant's heart, and her selfless attitude—which was soon to be displayed once again.

In the middle of the night, Doris awakened. Her son made sure she was comfortable and said, "Mom, look who is here. Jeff has come to be with you."

Doris turned, looked at me, and smiled. Then, in typical Doris fashion, she quietly asked, "Oh Jeff, why are you here? You have so many responsibilities and so many people depending on you. Don't worry about me, I'm fine. Any time you can get away from your work needs to be spent with your family, not me. But thank you for coming."

Tears welled in my eyes. Even facing death, Doris was thinking of others. She was more concerned about me than about herself. She was more interested in my family's well-being than her physical pain. She was still graciously grateful for the simple kindness of a personal visit. Doris had lived her life for others—and she was dying the same way. She believed the declaration in Philippians 1:21, "to live is Christ and to die is gain."

Spending the night in that hospital room is one of the highest and holiest moments of my four decades in pastoral ministry. Not remarkable because of anything I said or did, but because I was in the presence of someone so saturated with God's Spirit, God's Word, and God's presence, she exuded God's grace, power, peace, and hope.

Yes, hope, in the midst of dying. That's one of the great paradoxes of the Christian faith. We have hope, even in the midst of death. We have this hope because our faith rests on the reality our Founder conquered death when He was raised from the dead. Jesus died a brutal and real death. He tasted death just like every other person in the human race either has or will. He did not swoon or sleep or relax into some weird comatose state. He died. In the days after His death, His followers were bewildered and discouraged. They had invested so much in Jesus, and now He was dead. Really dead, and seemingly gone from their lives.

As we all know, three days later He overcame death, defeated it soundly, roaring out of the grave like the Lion of the Tribe of Judah He was prophesied to be. He erupted from the grave, fully alive and reigning in all His splendor and glory. Jesus ultimately ascended to heaven where He now sits at the right hand of God. Yes, he died. But, oh my, how He now lives!

This is the great hope of our faith. It's the reason my friend Doris reflected such peace, grace, and hope at the end of her life. She knew Jesus. She had experienced the benefit of His death—her conversion. Now she was about to experience the benefit of his resurrection—her own transition from temporal to eternal life. Her hope was fixed on Jesus.

As an aging grandfather, much closer to the end of life than the beginning, one of my remaining goals is to die well. For me, this means coming to the end of my life with the same convictions that have sustained me over the past fifty years as a believer. It also means clinging more and more to my true hope—the resurrected Jesus—and less and less to people, things, and ideas which offer false hope.

Everyone is looking for hope. Secular advertisers and marketers know this and use this longing to sell everything from clothes to cars. They assure us having the right things will give us hope. Other influencers take a higher road where hope is found in relationships. They assure us hope comes when we find the right person to make our lives complete.

Even those of us who have strong marriages and families know how transient and unpredictable these relationships can be. Finally, particularly in American culture, some believe hope is found in achievements. Conquering life brings hope— so they promise—but really these efforts just put us on a treadmill to nowhere.

Doris knew better. She had enjoyed fine cars and always dressed nicely. Her family and church relationships were enriching and meaningful. And, partnering with her husband, they had several noteworthy professional accomplishments and enjoyed the rewards of those endeavors. But Doris also had the wisdom to trust none of these things for her ultimate hope. She trusted Jesus instead.

Life is meant to be enjoyable. There's nothing wrong with appreciating possessions, relationships, and achievements. Just don't fall prey to the temptation any of these things will sustain you in this life or the next. Put your hope in Jesus. He will never fail you in life or in death. In the Bible, Paul wrote, "For me, to live is Christ and to die is gain." When you read this verse, substitute your name for the pronoun. Make Paul's claim your own.

For most, death is the most dreaded part of life. For Christians, it is a moment of profound hope. Doris modeled that for me and motivates me to fix my hopes where they belong— on Jesus. Let her story inspire you as well.

Jeff Iorg is the president of Gateway Seminary where he also teaches leadership, preaching, and church ministry courses.

Fearfully and Wonderfully Made

For you created my inmost being; you knit me
together in my mother's womb. I praise you because
I am fearfully and wonderfully made; your works are
wonderful, I know that full well.

—Psalm 139:13–14

I love children. They are a symbol of hope to me. No matter the family they were born into, or the struggles in life they experience, there is always hope. Hope to rise above their circumstances. Hope to become a great man or woman of God. Hope for an education. Hope for joy, love, and peace in their otherwise chaotic lives. Hope for people outside their families to pour into them.

Each baby is knitted together by God in their mother's womb. Each child is fearfully and wonderfully made, and through their lives, we see the hand of God and His work is wonderful. While we wish every child grew up in a loving Christian home, we know this is not true. While we wish for each of them to be safe, we know for some this is not true. But we do thank God for His love that can transform them from a baby into a child of God.

As a missionary in Africa, I saw every type of possible home life. I saw loving Christian homes where the Bible was read and where the children were taken to church. I saw loving grandparents raise their grandchildren as the children's parents had died of AIDS. I saw love exemplified as they sacrificed to put food on the table and clothes on their backs. I saw parents try to help their children with homework, even though the parents never went to school.

But I also saw children whose parents were alcoholics and stumbled home occasionally to sleep and would at times strike their children in their drunkenness. I saw tremendous hunger, as many families did good to get one meal a day. I saw homes where the oldest child of twelve was the caregiver of all the younger children, orphans from war, sickness, and poverty.

To be able to have a worship service during school on Friday afternoons, the principal said we could not share about God unless the children asked us questions. So we had little pieces of paper and the children wrote us questions. We received all kinds of questions, even marriage proposals for our daughter. Some of the heartbreaking questions included: "Your mother drink alcohol you father died what would you do?" "Will you pray for me because at home I abused." "How can I belong to church when parents do not want me to go?" "Why did God not come see us?" But we did see the children accept Christ and their lives were changed.

For every heartache in a child's life, we would see hope in churches that loved the neighborhood children. We saw Christian coaches who worked tirelessly to coach basketball. Through sports they would share the love of God. I saw a Christian principal allowing missionaries to come on the school property and help with a school garden, lead an afterschool homework program and a worship service. During these school worship services, the children would sing praise to God like there was no tomorrow. I saw a national pastor take in twenty-five children whose parents had died of AIDS. He loved them as his own, even starting a garden at age seventy-three to feed these children.

After fourteen years of living in Africa, we transitioned to the United States. Our hearts broke as we said good-bye to all these children and the families and pastors we loved. We had hope because we had seen firsthand the love of the pastors, fellow missionaries, and Christian teachers and principals. We saw hope in a country with the highest AIDS rate and highest crime rates in the world. God is there. God brings hope in despair. He has fearfully and wonderfully created people in this country who would carry the banner of hope.

After moving to the US, we settled in a small community and my husband served as pastor. We felt led to the church because of their bus ministry on Wednesday nights. They fed the children and youth who came from unchurched homes and then loved on these kids through crafts, Bible study, recreation, and prayer. The buses ran in the snow and the rain.

I grew very close to these children. One boy lived with his great-grandmother, as his mother and grandmother were in prison due to drugs. I started a choir thinking the parents would come to hear their children sing in church. Out of more than fifty children, only a few parents would come. I would see the children strain their eyes looking for their parents, only to discover they hadn't come.

I grew very close to Elizabeth* and Scott.* Their grandparents were in prison for drugs. Their parents were divorced and they were passed between Mom and Dad. Elizabeth told me she had a large hole in her floor and it was scary to get up in the night, as she was afraid she would fall through. I was never allowed inside. I "adopted" Elizabeth and Scott. They came to my house regularly. I sat with them at church and always had a bag of quiet toys and coloring sheets for them to use during the sermon. I gave them food and clothes. I worked at their school and greeted them daily. I loved them dearly.

As I realized their upbringing and home life, my heart would ache profusely. I grieved with every story they told me of their home. But slowly, I began to see hope change their lives. They got more confident. Scott, who was behind in school, began to compete in Special Olympics and win. He learned to read and talk. Elizabeth took pride in her appearance and sang loudly in our children's choir, even joining the adult choir as a child.

Most of the children would have "church parents" who particularly loved them. They were fed before choir and Bible study as it is sure hard to learn on an empty stomach. We started the backpack ministry to give them food on the weekend. I saw lives changed as they accepted Christ and were baptized. They were loved and their lives were transformed.

It doesn't matter if you live in poverty and hopelessness from Africa or the United States. God can put people in your life and use them to bring hope. Jesus can transform lives. Nothing is out of the range of God's love. There is always hope. Remember to search in life for those who need His hope.

Amy Boone is the executive director and treasurer of North Carolina Woman's Missionary Union.

*names changed

Follow Me

"Come, follow Me," Jesus said, "and I will send you out
to fish for people."

—Matthew 4:19

Fishing is a common trade in the Philippines where I grew up. It is hard work that requires long hours out on a blue moon in the middle of the sea, patiently casting nets and waiting for a good catch. I still remember waking up in the early morning over the weekend to watch how the fishermen pull their nets slowly to the shore with the expectation of catching lots of fish.

This is precisely what is going on here when Jesus asked Peter and Andrew, while casting their net into the sea of Galilee, to "follow Him" and come "fish for people." The call "to follow" will forever change their lives and the course of the world for people searching for hope.

My desire to follow Christ started way back as a young boy growing up in the province of Pangasinan in the 1980s. My family was a devout member of the Roman Catholic faith. I was raised to adhere to all the religious traditions and practices to bring honor and blessings to the entire family. I served as an altar boy to a local parish to assure this quest of favor and even aspired to enter the priesthood. In obedience to my parents, I faithfully performed my duties in assisting our local priest in my hometown for every Catholic Mass. My parents took pride in me as an altar boy, and my family gained favor and respect in the community. But was I following the real Christ or just following my family's religion?

I struggled to find real answers, especially on whether I knew Christ personally as my Lord. Even doing good works for people and serving in my local parish was not giving me answers to what I was looking for. So, I just kept performing, going with the flow of obeying all traditions and religious practices to hopefully assure me of eternal hope. It was a quest for truth from a wrong place because the answer can only be found in Christ and not from religion.

But one day, a good friend invited me to a Bible study where I heard the message of hope in Jesus Christ for the first time—that He died for my sins and promised eternal life if only I believed in Him. The gospel message of hope led me to repent from all my sins and place my faith in Jesus as my Lord and my Savior. Now, I was no longer following a religion but instead a real Savior in Jesus Christ. To know Him is to have eternal life. He's now constantly calling me to "follow Him" and surrender my entire life "to fish for people" in advancing His kingdom.

The call from Christ to "follow Him" was not easy at all. My parents and siblings were not in support of my newfound faith in Christ. To them, it was foolishness and an invitation to disgrace and dishonor the family. How much more when I tried asking permission from my parents to enroll in a Baptist seminary as I prepared for ministry.

I still remember the exact words my father told me: "From now on, you're on your own," while my mother cried and tried to convince me not to leave. That day, I left home to "follow Him" without my parents' blessings and the support of my siblings. My parents were heartbroken because of my obedience to God's calling. It was not easy to endure the pain of leaving my parents to follow Him.

The day arrived in the early 1990s when I graduated from seminary and was called to serve as a pastor in my hometown in the province. God not only allowed me to know Him in my church but also gave me the privilege to serve as their pastor. My ministry was now close to home, and I had opportunities to witness to my parents and siblings about Christ and what He had done in my life.

This time, the pain of leaving home because of "following Christ" turned into hope. By His sovereign grace, God saved my parents and siblings one after the other through my ministry. In addition, God gave me the privilege to share the gospel with my family and baptize some of them. As a result, there was not only me who followed Christ to become a "fisher of men," but four others of my immediate family responded to His call of "follow Me." Five of us now are serving in full-time ministry.

Today, I continue to "follow Him" and "fish for people" who need the gospel of hope. It might be painful for a while, but it's worth seeing how God turns pain into a joyful hope for others to know Christ. My story of "following Christ" started in the Philippines, but never ended there. It continued to Philadelphia, now in Nashville, and wherever God will call me to "fish for people."

The question is, Will you follow Him? You might experience momentary pain, but it's worth everything in exchange for eternal hope for others.

Peter Yanes is the executive director of Asian American relations and mobilization for the Southern Baptist Convention.

If You Know Him, You Trust Him

When I am afraid, I put my trust in you.

—Psalm 56:3

One thing we all have in common is that if we are alive, we will have trials and tribulations. There will be situations beyond our control that will cause us to lean heavily on our faith. Have you found yourself calling on the Lord more and more each day? Are you currently afraid of what tomorrow may bring? Well, let me encourage you. God can and will meet you right where you are in this very moment.

Imagine you are a fourteen-year-old high school freshman member of the marching band color guard, and you and your brother, a varsity football player, have just returned home from a Friday night football game. Your parents, ever-present diehard fans of the football team, also attended the out-of-town game and have not yet arrived home. You receive a phone call to drive to your grandmother's house, where you subsequently learn your parents have been in a bad car accident. They were involved in a head-on collision where a drunk driver crossed the center line and struck the vehicle driven by your dad on the driver's side.

One of your first feelings is likely that of fear. You fear for the safety and well-being of your parents, and you fear for what the future may hold for them and for you. You question the events of the night and if there was some way you could have prevented the accident. Because of the seriousness of the wreck, you beg the Lord for more time with your parents. You go through a series of emotions, including regret, as you ask the Lord to forgive you for any disrespect, typical of a teenager, that you have ever shown to your parents or to Him.

I was that teenager. That Friday night in September and during the long road of recovery that lay ahead for my parents, I experienced fear like I had never known. Fortunately, throughout my life, my mother had insisted that I enter the doors of our small Baptist church every time they were open, and I knew of Jesus Christ. I had been told of His many miracles, His healing power, His burden to feed the hungry and heal the sick, and His death, burial, and resurrection. I knew the Lord and had to trust Him to heal and to take care of my parents. This situation was out of my control, but from what I learned of the Lord in Sunday School, I knew Him, and I had to trust Him.

In Psalm 56:3, David says, "When I am afraid, I put my trust in you." David, the youngest of Jesse's sons and the teenaged shepherd boy who was anointed by Samuel to become king, is described as a man after God's own heart in the Bible. This same David, who defeated the giant Goliath and was a successful leader in Israel's army, also admitted to being afraid. In this scripture, he does not say *if* he becomes afraid, but he says *when* he is afraid, he chooses to trust the Lord.

Sometimes, when we fear something, we think about that fear until it seems to take over our lives. We do not sleep or eat, and after a while, we cannot even seem to think of anything else but that thing that is standing in our way. It occupies our minds, directs our actions and how we treat each other, and even causes us to forget those lessons learned in Sunday School or the words of hymns, like " 'Tis So Sweet to Trust in Jesus." We tend to focus more on the problem than on the Problem Solver. However, if we know Him, then we must trust Him.

We get to know more about God, His character, and His love for us by spending time with Him. As we study the Bible, spend time in prayer, worship Him corporately and privately, serve

Him by serving others, and fellowship with other believers, our relationship with the Lord grows stronger and our faith goes to new levels. When those trials and tribulations come to test our faith, we can respond like David and acknowledge the fear but turn the situation over to the Lord by trusting Him to handle it.

The situation with my parents' accident was totally out of my control, but the Lord demonstrated His power in the healing of my dad and mom. My father was left paralyzed from the waist down after that accident but accepted the Lord as his personal Savior and experienced the gift of salvation during his healing process. My mother lost a few teeth in the accident but gained a saved husband and renewed marriage with God as the head.

Our family unit experienced unity, in the name of Jesus, as never before. Generations to come will know of Jesus Christ because of the struggles and faith of my family that began that Friday night in September. I could not have planned that outcome if I had tried. I am grateful that even amid my fear, the Lord loved me and gave me a personal testimony of faith and trust. I grew in my faith in God and began to live with a renewed hope in Christ.

Today, as you consider all that is going on around you, the things that may be happening to you, and the stumbling blocks that may be in your way, I want you to reflect on the life of David and especially his words in Psalm 56:3. God is our refuge and our strength, an ever-present help in the time of trouble. If you know Him, then you trust Him.

Tamiko Jones is the executive director and treasurer of WMU of Texas.

Mirror, Mirror, on the Wall

Praise be to the LORD my Rock, who trains my hands for war, my fingers for battle.

—Psalm 144:1

Mirrors are deceiving. There are mirrors such as a lipstick mirror, that only reflects one small part of an entire body. There are magnifying mirrors making what is small look huge. There are mirrors purposefully designed to cause the onlooker to appear thinner. Nonetheless, we rely on them. Sometimes, the mirrors we rely on are the mirrors of culture, people, ads, or social media. Distorted mirrors are ever before us. Is there a perfect mirror? Yes! God's Word!

Psalm 139:14 declares we are fearfully and wonderfully made, a lesson David, the author of this Psalm, learned as a shepherd boy in a few of his own battles. In one, he defeated a lion and a bear. The success of that battle gave him the courage to face his next, a standoff with Goliath.

Goliath was a giant Philistine. When David encountered Goliath, he found him ridiculing the God of Israel while the army of Israel cowered in fear. David was in shock. Why would they allow a Philistine to say such things about the Lord? With the courage of a mighty warrior, David approached the king of Israel, Saul, offering to take on Goliath and defend the name of the Lord. Saul had a list of reasons why David would fail, but in the end, Saul offered his armor and wished him Godspeed. The armor made sense for Saul, but for David it was too big, heavy, and cumbersome. As the story is told, David made the choice to rely on what he knew as a shepherd, his slingshot and God's power. Where does your hope lie?

For David to have continued in Saul's armor would have been pretending he was someone he was not. He would have been rejecting God's design for that of Saul.

If David had faced Goliath in Saul's armor, he most likely would have lost the battle. Instead, he capitalized on the talent God had endowed him with, the ability to throw a stone. It seems so simple, but in reality, it took much faith. A small simple stone as compared to magnificent armor makes no logistical sense. However, it is not the logistics of the armor that wins battles, it is the One who endows them that brings victory. God has gifted each one of us for a specific purpose and the ability to face every Goliath with the expectation of victory.

What is a Goliath? A Goliath may show up in the form of low self-esteem, a struggling marriage, a wayward child, a learning-impaired child, parents, health, ministry, aging, grandchildren. The list is endless.

What is Saul's armor? It may be in the form of busyness, perfection, comparison, and most tragic of all, a veneer of religion rather than a relationship with the Savior. For me, Saul's armor came in the form of a fellow missionary that I admired. Homeschool for her was no less than five hours. I struggled with thirty minutes! Her sons always took off their shoes before entering their house. My white tile floors were barely visible through the dirty footprints. Her sons had perfectly white socks. My sons were fortunate to find a sock, clean was optional. Needless to say, I was miserable.

Even worse, I was making life for my family miserable. In the mirror I was using, I did not see myself as the fairest in the land. Like David, I needed to lay down "Saul's armor" and rely on God's wisdom in creating me to be me. Like David, looking back allowed me to see all the ways God had prepared me for my battles. The me God saved despite my childhood in a non-Christian dysfunctional home. The me who was right for my family.

As I look back on my life, there have been Goliaths to face. Some of them came with tragedies and struggles that showed up in the lives of our three sons. Others showed up in my own life. I shudder to think of the loss that could have occurred had I stayed in someone else's armor. It would have been great.

There are some elements of armor that each of us as believers possess: The Armor of God (Ephesians 6:11), salvation (John 3:16), the Fruit of the Spirit (Galatians 5:22–23). It is our gifts, talents, past, personality traits, strengths, and weaknesses, when added to the givens, that are in place to prepare us for the battles and Goliaths each of us will face. Rest assured God is in the details and promises victory.

What I learned as a five-year-old when camping prepared me for life on the mission field spending days at a time in villages with no electricity, running water, or plumbing of any kind. What I learned from attending thirteen schools in twelve years prepared me for the moving that comes with mission life. The uphill battles prepared me to equip our sons for their uphill battles. The dysfunctional home I knew as a child taught me a lot about how to have grace as an adult. My testimony as the daughter of an alcoholic was the game changer for a young man who was in the middle of what was behind me. Every amazing act of God I have seen prepared me to step out in faith when called to the next battlefield. My past, present, and future story is only a tool in my armor to be used when I face another Goliath. That gives me hope.

Whatever is behind you, in front of you, or ahead of you, take heart. You have been well prepared for battle, down to the tiniest of details.

After twenty-two years with IMB and WMU, Gayla Parker currently serves as adjunct professor at Ouachita Baptist University and the executive director of the Pregnancy Resource Center for Southwest Arkansas.

Walking Through the Worst Bad Days

But those who hope in the LORD will renew their
strength. They will soar on wings like eagles; they will
run and not grow weary, they will walk and not be faint.

—Isaiah 40:31

January 5, 1996, was the worst bad day. It wasn't the first bad day, or the last bad day, but in all the schemes, slings, and arrows that daily life brings, it was epically bad.

And I would discover that hope hangs around when the worst bad day ends.

Fridays were busy at work at the Missouri Baptist Convention where I was a young staffer tasked with writing, photography, and page layout for the *Word & Way*, the news journal of the convention at that time. The evening ahead, my boyfriend and I planned to avoid the bitter cold and play a card game with another couple, his high school friends.

Even though it was a quarter of a century ago, I remember well the tiny apartment I found when I took the job, on the same street as my office—the wacky kitchen with watermelon-red countertops, harvest-gold stove, avocado-green fridge, bright pink phone, and old-fashioned landline.

As the workday drifted into early dusk, like happens in the dead of winter, I drove up the steep hill from the office and parked on the side street, like I did every day. Walked up the sidewalk. Opened the front door. A few minutes later, I answered the ringing phone.

One minute, life was "before." The next, life was "after." After I learned that my dad—my stepdad who had provided for me as long as I could remember, who attended every youth group function, every basketball game and track meet across the Oklahoma Panhandle . . . my dad who swatted me seven times one day when I was about eight (that was also a bad day of my own fault), who set an example of memorizing God's Word, who made the best homemade Halloween costumes (a robot! a toilet!) . . . my dad who taught me how to fix a flat tire, who taught his son and four daughters how to hang sheetrock and finish wood, how to drive go-carts . . . my dad who represented the community as Santa at the holiday bazaar, as a volunteer firefighter, as Rotary president . . . my dad was gone.

"Gone how?" I asked. "Left?"

"He shot himself in the garage workshop."

"Was it an accident?"

"No."

The very worst of the bad day was not the surprise. I believe shock is a gift of God to get us through the unimaginable moments that otherwise would shatter us. The worst was not his departure, his abandonment. Essentially, I'd lost my first dad to divorce when I was three, and it was terrible to lose another father I love. But the worst—the very worst of the worst bad day—was knowing my dad had been so tortured without hope.

Hope is the breath of chilly air when the stifling world is closing in. Hope is the fuel to get through another weary, drought-ridden mile of life. Hope is the mercy of Christ that pours over oppressive self-doubt and shame.

January 6, 1996, was a pretty bad day too. A severe ice storm grounded flights and blocked roads. I couldn't get home. I wallowed in bed. There was no "soaring on wings like eagles," for me that day, no "running and not growing weary."

We didn't see eagles often (if ever) at the dusty end of Oklahoma. But occasionally we would see them when Dad took us camping in the Rocky Mountains. They are austere and grand, they represent power and freedom. Years later, I'd learn that eagles have amazing eyesight, detecting prey up to two miles away. Eagles have strong fidelity and sturdy nests. Their wings, some sources say, are stronger pound-for-pound than an airplane wing.

And eagles rarely flap their mighty wings. They conserve their energy by catching an updraft to gain altitude. While other birds may give chase, flapping and squawking in pursuit, eagles have a secret weapon which outpaces their predators. They catch an air current and outpace their shadows.

Hope placed in the Lord, Isaiah tells us, renews our strength, so we can mount up—ascend out of life's valleys into its heights—on wings like eagles. On wings that are majestically engineered to outpace the shadows.

As I made it home for the funeral, set for a frozen Tuesday, there was one thing people said to me over and over: How are you making it through this? Your family is showing such peace, such calm. The only truthful answer: My hope is in the Lord.

Why? God's gracious love has wrapped around me, bringing me peace that passes all human understanding. Over, and over, and over. I have lived and learned that there is nothing better than to place my hope in God.

Believers do not grieve as those with no hope.

My dad knew the importance of instilling God's Word in his children and insisting we stay connected to our church community. Years later, I was told our friends thought he was the strictest dad in town. (It felt like it when I was a teenager!) But twenty-five years later, while his kids have faced plenty of challenges, all five still have our hope rooted in the Lord each day. To soar, or maybe to run, or often just to walk.

My dad knew in his heart, but forgot in his mind that day, to hope in the Lord. Are you feeling hopeless, in despair? Help is available. Please talk to someone today.

Julie McGowan is the associate vice president of communications and public relations for the International Mission Board.

National Suicide Prevention Lifeline: 800-273-8255

How Far Can Our Light Shine?

In the same way, let your light shine before others,
that they may see your good deeds and praise your
Father in heaven.

—Matthew 5:16

A few years ago, I was present when a ten-year-old boy prayed and asked Jesus to come into his life to be his Lord and Savior. At his request, we planned for him to be baptized in Lake DeGray near his hometown of Arkadelphia, Arkansas. He wanted to be baptized there because he thought his friends on the baseball team were more likely to attend, and he wanted his baptism to be a testimony and witness to what Jesus meant to him. We planned the baptism date for a Sunday afternoon in June, but there was a conflict that forced us to postpone until a later date.

After yet another conflict, we finally settled on the perfect Sunday afternoon and met at the lake. Just like he planned, and we had prayed for, his teammates were present along with their parents and several of his family members.

As the two of us waded out into the lake, and as the boy's family and friends watched from the shore, I noticed a group of Hispanics swimming about twenty yards away from us. They immediately stood still in the water, and one of their group on shore turned down the music that had been blasting over the speaker.

After the baptism, and as we waded out of the water back to shore, I walked over to the Hispanic group just to thank them for their consideration and respect. Being a Spanish speaker, I greeted them and thanked them in Spanish. One of the young men said to me in Spanish, "Was that a baptism?"

"Yes," I said.

He then said to me as his right hand patted his chest, "That really touched me."

The Spanish word *tocar* means both "touch" and "knock (on a door)." I briefly explained to him the meaning and symbolism of the death, burial, and resurrection of Jesus and explained the salvation decision that the boy had made. I thanked him again for their courtesy and respect, shook his hand, and walked back up the hill to celebrate with the boy, the baseball team, and the parents.

After about fifteen minutes and a few cupcakes, and when my clothes were partially dry, I said goodbye to the group and walked to my truck in the parking area. When I took off my wet shoes, I heard someone walk up behind me. I turned around and was surprised to see the young Hispanic man had followed me to my truck.

He asked me to again explain to him why the boy was baptized and what that really meant. He said for the second time, "For real, that really touched me."

For the next several minutes, we talked about what it means to have a personal relationship with Jesus. I shared with him Revelation 3:20 in which Jesus says, "Behold, I stand at the door and knock [touch]" (NKJV). I explained, "When we hear that 'touch,' and open the door of our heart, He will enter our lives and begin a personal relationship that changes us for all of eternity." The young man became increasingly interested as we talked about how Jesus changes us from the inside out, that our old life will be buried with Christ, that all our sin will be forgiven, and that we will receive new life . . . that "old things will pass away, and all things will be made new" (2 Corinthians 5:17). I then said to him it seemed very obvious to me that Jesus was "touching" the door of his heart, and that there would never be a better time than that moment for him to call upon the name of the Lord and be saved. We prayed a simple prayer together, and he invited Jesus to take control of his life.

There are some unforgettable things about that Sunday afternoon encounter at a lake in southwest Arkansas. The young, Hispanic man's name was Jesus. He and his friends were from Mexico City and had come to Arkansas on vacation. While staying in Little Rock, someone told them that coming to Lake DeGray would be a nice day trip. This was the last day of their vacation. On that particular day, at that particular time, on that particular lake, and at that particular beach, a ten-year-old boy who had decided to follow Jesus, wanted his baptism to be a witness to his friends. He wanted his friends to know Jesus like he knew Jesus, and God used the desire of that boy's heart to "touch" the heart of a vacationing Hispanic man who was so "touched" that his life is forever changed.

What an encouragement to know we live with the hope (confident expectation) that when we are prompted by God to let our "light shine before others," He has already gone to great lengths to prepare the maximum impact of that light. The desire of a ten-year-old to let his light shine can reach across culture, language, and nations, and I can personally testify that it can cause you to "glorify your Father in heaven" (Matthew 5:16).

Stan Parris is a retired pastor-missions pastor living in Arkadelphia, Arkansas.

Where Is the Love?

But I tell you, love your enemies and pray for those
who persecute you.

—Matthew 5:44

My growing up years were recorded by the songs my brother and I listened to on the radio as we fell asleep each night. To this day, things happen, and songs start playing through my mind. In recent days, echoes of the old Roberta Flack song, "Where Is the Love," came flooding into my mind as I was contemplating these days of controversy, anger, and hatred. I searched for the lyrics and found the question asked again, by the Black Eyed Peas in 2009: "Send some guidance from above . . . (Where's the love?)"

Well, the Father has sent us some "guidance from above!" He sent it wrapped in human flesh, His very own Son, Jesus. He taught us to love and then demonstrated the fullness of His love at the cross. The love He taught us was supernatural and world changing. He told us, "Love one another. As I have loved you, so you must love one another. By this everyone will know that you are my disciples if you love one another" (John 13:34–35).

What passes for love in our culture is generally conditional love. If you live up to my expectations, I'll "love" you. If you give me what I want, then I will "love" you. "I love you" can be so twisted that it too often means, "I love myself and you give me what I want to make me happy."

That is not biblical love. That's self-centeredness. Such transactional love is not love at all—it's just love of self. We "love" someone for what they do for us. If they quit performing to our expectations, we don't "love" them anymore. Such is the failure of many marriages.

We are all broken, messed up, and hard to love. We're like porcupines trying to connect, but we keep poking each other and hurting each other. Jesus taught and lived a different kind of love. Agape love is never self-centered (1 Corinthians 13) but is instead about giving ourselves to others. Agape love gives itself, its time, its devotion, its attention, its everything to the beloved. Love values the beloved; love strives to please the beloved; love serves the beloved. Love values someone else over our self-interest. Such love is difficult and rare.

Jesus teaches us how to love others by building on a rich tradition of biblical and Jewish thought regarding human relationships. I have found it helpful to understand His extraordinary teaching on love by following several steps of refinement: the Silver Rule, the Golden Rule, the Platinum Rule, and finally, Jesus' ultimate statement of love, what I call the Diamond Rule (Matthew 5:44).

The Silver Rule: The Silver Rule is a negative statement of the Golden Rule, "Do not do unto others what you do not want done unto you." This was a step up from the *lex talionis* of the Old Testament, an eye for any eye, a tooth for a tooth, which simply limited revenge. According to tradition, the Silver Rule was articulated in the first century BC and associated with the development of the Jewish Mishnah and the Talmud, a sort of commentary on the Torah and its law.

The Golden Rule: Jesus restated the Silver Rule by expressing it in a positive way. "Therefore, whatever you want men to do to you, do also to them, for this is the Law and the Prophets" (Matthew 7:12 NKJV). It has popularly been rendered, "Do unto others as you would have them do unto you." Treat other people the way you would like to be treated. As profound as this teaching is, it is not the pinnacle of Jesus' teaching on love. In many ways, this kind of love can be a business transaction with an expectation of reciprocating respect.

The Platinum Rule: Jesus further refined our understanding of love when He clarified that we are to love everyone we encounter, "Love your neighbor as yourself" (Matthew 22:39). I've heard people say this implies we are to love ourselves, but that was not Jesus' point. We naturally look out for ourselves. Jesus wanted us to understand our obligation to look out for our neighbors—anyone and everyone. He followed up this rule with the story of the Good Samaritan, "Which of these three [the pastor, the church leader, or the despised man] do you think proved to be a neighbor to the man who fell into the hands of the robbers?" (Luke 10:36). Too many of us are physically mature but emotionally three-year-olds who believe the world revolves around us. Jesus reminds us that we are to care as much about our neighbors as we do about ourselves.

The Diamond Rule: In Matthew 5:43–44 Jesus expands this call to love in an extraordinary way; I call this the Diamond Rule of love. Not only are we called upon to love our neighbors, we are also called to love our enemies. Are you kidding? This is the ultimate test of love. A test Jesus, Himself, passed.

Jesus illustrated the Diamond Rule, real love, at the cross, "But God proves his own love for us in that while we were still sinners, Christ died for us" (Romans 5:8 CSB). He loved us while we were still in rebellion against God—while we were still His enemies (Romans 8:7). That's the Diamond Rule in action. The Diamond Rule is not for wimps. It takes character of steel to live like this. That's exactly what Jesus showed us at the cross, "Father, forgive them for they know not what they are doing" (Luke 23:34). This is the ultimate kind of love; love your enemies.

I have always been challenged by the lyrics of a Dionne Warwick song: "What the world needs now is love, sweet love." She is so right. What the world needs now is love, sweet love— lived out by those of us who have experienced the love of Jesus and want to pass it on (pun intended, another song from my youth). Where is the love? I pray the world can experience it through you and me. Such love has the power to transform a hopeless and broken world.

Leo Endel is the executive director of Minnesota-Wisconsin Baptist Convention.

Good News for Everyone

Everyone who calls on the name of the
Lord will be saved.

—Romans 10:13

One of the marks of our American society is our strong independence, doing things ourselves, the idea of self-reliance. Alexis de Tocqueville defined the "individualism" arising from this independence as one of the top five values critical to America's success.

In 1835, Alexis de Tocqueville, a French political philosopher and historian, published the first volume of *Democracy in America*. His analysis of the political system in the United States became the book as a result of his travels throughout the United States from 1831 to 1832. *Democracy in America* analyzed how democracy impacted every aspect of life in the US. Tocqueville observed how democracy created a strong sense of individualism. He also noted that, unlike in Europe, there were no hierarchical societal classes, women and children were more independent, and freedom of religion allowed for more religious denominations.

Obviously, Americans have an extremely independent spirit that has helped shape this country and helped us achieve a great many successes. However, while independence and self-reliance may be valuable characteristics to have in some arenas of life, they are not sufficient when it comes to spiritual matters.

Throughout history, mankind has tried to perform or be "good enough" to warrant divine favor. We have developed sets of rules and pathways that we hope would be pleasing to God. We have tried to independently earn our salvation.

My wife, Kathy, and I served as missionaries in Brazil, and this is what we observed when we landed there: a profoundly spiritual people trying so many things to earn their salvation. They were very religiously observant, but many were missing an assurance of salvation and a personal relationship with Jesus Christ. Seeing this, we took every opportunity to share alongside our Brazilian Baptist Convention brothers and sisters. The evangelistic theme being used at that time was "So Jesus Christo Salva"—"Only Jesus Christ Saves."

One week, while out doing an evangelistic campaign, a young woman came up during the invitation. After the service, as my wife and visiting mission volunteers were talking with people and I was busy putting away the projector and film, I glanced around and saw the young woman talking with my wife. I stopped and joined them.

Marilena began to tell us her story. "All my life," she said, "I have wanted to know God." Looking up into a night sky filled with thousands of stars, she continued to speak. "When I look into the heavens and see the beautiful stars, I know there must be a God who put them there. And when I stand on the rocks and look out over the beautiful ocean, I know there must be a God who created this beauty. One day I went to my parents and asked them about God," she said, "but they didn't know what to say."

Marilena even walked seven miles to the closest church and spoke to a priest in her search for God. "He told me many things, but I could not understand them," she said in a low, sad voice.

Then Marilena turned to me, her face brightening. "Tonight," she said, "when the volunteers shared the difference Jesus had made in their lives and when I heard you preach the gospel, my heart understood. I accepted Jesus as my Savior and Lord." With happy tears streaming down her face, and with one of the biggest smiles I've ever seen, she said, "Thank you. Thank you for coming to tell me about Jesus."

We believe everyone who calls on the name of the Lord will be saved. We believe this good news is for everyone, everywhere. Our churches preach and our International Mission Board has as its vision statement: "A multitude from every nation, tribe, people and language, knowing and worshiping our Lord Jesus Christ" (see Revelation 7:9). We are committed to do all we can to see that this good news is shared around the world.

There are people in your community and around the world still waiting for someone to come and tell them this good news. There are people in your community and mine who think they can earn their salvation, or that it is something that can be passed down like an heirloom. They have not been presented with the true gospel message that Jesus has paid it all. We don't have to earn it.

We need to truly recognize our need of salvation and ask Christ to forgive our sins, to be our Savior and Lord. Let's continue to pray, give, go, and send. Let's share the good news that everyone who calls on the name of the Lord will be saved.

Terry Sharp is a convention and network relations leader and coleader diaspora coalition for the International Mission Board.

Sheep Among Wolves

I am sending you out like sheep among wolves.
Therefore be as shrewd as snakes and as
innocent as doves.

—Matthew 10:16

No one wants to get eaten up by a wolf. If Jesus was trying to give his disciples a hopeful pep talk, I'm not sure this would have encouraged them much. Yet, Jesus never was one to beat around the bush. He wanted them to be prepared for what they might face as they went out on their own to proclaim the good news of the kingdom.

As I look over this passage in Matthew, I find something interesting. He tells them to avoid the Gentiles and Samaritans during this outreach trip. I thought they would be the wolves, but no, it's the Jews, their own people who would rise up against them, hand them over to councils, and flog them in synagogues, among their own people where they needed to be as shrewd as snakes and innocent as doves.

After spending more than twenty years among a people "not my own," I get Jesus' point. When we serve in cross-cultural settings, people are drawn to us because we're different. We're different because of Christ, yes, but we're also different because of race, language, lifestyle, and worldview. In many ways, God uses the differences to draw people to ask questions and thus allow us to build bridges to the gospel.

These last ten years back among "my people" have proved a difficult challenge. Because I look like them, they expect me to talk like them, live like them, and have the same worldview. Thirty years ago, that might have proved easier, but not only have I changed, but my home culture has changed. I sometimes feel more the foreigner in my own hometown than I did in the Middle East, and it's not just because I've lived overseas and have a wider worldview. No, it's because God has been pushed aside or relegated to a place of little significance, not only in the world at large, but sometimes in the church.

I go back to Jesus' words—we should always go back to His words. Just prior to this statement about sheep and wolves, He's teaching them that it's important to rely on Him for the journey. When we make the plan, something is bound to go wrong, but when we trust His plan, He'll use even rejection to be a statement for his lordship in our life.

Now we come to how He's sending us out as sheep among wolves. The Jews of the first century were so bound by the law they'd forgotten God. They'd put aside God's Word for man-made traditions and teachings. Their identity depended on their adherence to the Law of Moses more than the covenant established by God.

Jesus disrupted their narrative.

Not much has changed in the twenty-first century. Narratives still matter, and people will push back against anything that forces them to question it. When we served in the Middle East, one of the greatest ways to gain a breakthrough with a Muslim was to get him or her to question Islam. They'd grown up all their lives not able or even willing to question what they were taught. The religious establishment was everything and to go against it meant blasphemy, becoming an outcast, and sometimes even death—still does.

I find the same is true in our own culture today. When questioning a narrative means you question the spirit of the age, then something is wrong, and the wolves come out. That's why the sheep (believers) have become mute—we don't want to get eaten up!

But Jesus doesn't want us mute. We have a message to share, and it's a good one at that. Just like He sent the twelve out on that test-run outreach trip, He's pushing us out of our comfort zones. When He does, we find ourselves face-to-face with wolves. So, how do we disrupt the narrative without getting eaten?

We become shrewd sheep.

Wondering what that means? According to Wordnik. com, *shrewd* means: "having or showing a clever awareness or resourcefulness, especially in practical matters." I can't think of anything more practical than work for the kingdom of God, can you? I like that first clue about shrewdness—a clever awareness. Are you aware of what's going on around you, these days? We can no longer claim the "I'm just a dumb sheep, relying on my shepherd" trick. It's not going to work, and Jesus doesn't let us play dumb.

Be aware.

For me, after twenty years away from my country, I had to try to figure out what was going on all over again. Talk about reverse culture shock. I had no idea what had happened to my country while I was away, so I started listening to what people said, reading books, and watching the news. As Christ followers, we cannot stick our heads in the sand to what the spirit of the age is doing, because it's happening in our own backyards, our own homes, and even our own churches.

Be resourceful.

A snake learns how to get around, even in tight places. It can also blend into the environment, invisible to its prey or attacker but for different reasons. For the last ten years I've worked in a secular environment, and if there's any place that makes me feel like a sheep among wolves, it's at work. It's not because my co-workers are mean or attack me, but because we think differently, look at the world differently, and respond to crises differently. If anything, I've learned how to keep quiet, earn their respect, and choose when to speak truth into their lives. Being resourceful means we wait to speak or act until the Spirit tells us.

An innocent sheep is a clean sheep.

When I lived in West Africa, I watched a white and fluffy lamb follow its mother down the street. Life can rub off on us, and when we're not alert and aware of our surroundings, we can easily lose our innocence as sheep of the Good Shepherd. That's why we have to keep our accounts clean with the Lord.

A life of integrity is a huge draw for those living the lie.

When the world around us sees us face trials with dignity and grace, they begin to question the narrative—think three guys in a fiery furnace. How are we working to demonstrate a life of purity and integrity to those around us? Do we live the hope we profess?

Being a shrewd and innocent sheep doesn't guarantee an easy life.

If the events of the last few years have taught us anything, they should teach us that it's not going to get any better. Jesus said all this and more would happen. The wolves are all around us, but instead of reverting to the corner of your sheep pen, yield to the Shepherd's push to go out and live a life of integrity and witness.

Carol Ghattas served over twenty years with the International Mission Board and is presently the branch manager of Linebaugh Public Library in Murfreesboro, Tennessee.

Great Is My Hopefulness

Because of the Lᴏʀᴅ's great love we are not consumed,
for his compassions never fail. They are new every
morning; great is your faithfulness.

—Lamentations 3:22–23

On February 18, 2019, my precious wife of more than thirty-five years collapsed and died with no warning. One sentence of a few words changed my life. However, I learned that those excruciating words did not change my Father's faithfulness.

The moment the news was spoken out loud to me, my world began plummeting. It seemed as if I were being consumed. My eyes and heart were telling me I was being devoured. Sight was not my friend. This intense onslaught began in an instant, but it was not going anywhere, anytime soon. Instead, confusion cascaded in upon me. Everything in my line of sight was warped and distorted. The pain moved in and set up residence like an illegal squatter.

One sweet life companion. One sudden heartbreaking loss. Ongoing, pervasive, and unspeakable pain. I learned not to diminish my loss. Loss is difficult.

I learned quickly I could not avoid the pain, nor should I avoid the deepening injury that accompanied my loss. I have learned, likewise, you cannot sidestep the ongoing pain you're facing. If you're in pain, do not pull away. Do not diminish the ramifications of your loss. Instead, press into Christ and His gospel to learn the lessons of hope He longs to teach you.

Your pain may be great. But great, also, is your hopefulness. Your faith will deepen, if you address your loss appropriately when walking through painful loss.

Your loving Father seeks to teach you deep, soul-enriching lessons. The Savior promises to walk with you in intimacy. Immanuel, God is with us.

But first, you learn that brokenness is worse than you knew.

Throw off any illusions and recognize our world is broken. Death and loss are manifestations of the horrible plague known as the fall of man. Temporal death and loss are shadows of eternal death and loss. In pain, God seeks to communicate that brokenness is worse than you knew. Brokenness is all around you. And it's across the whole world. We have a part to play in addressing brokenness with the hope of the gospel.

Brokenness is worse than you knew.

The brokenness of the world cost the Father His Son. Brokenness is that serious. It cost the life of God to overwhelm the affliction of loss. But now, death is eternally defeated, and friendship with God is heralded in the gospel.

His love is deeper and greater than you knew.

Facing my own loss resembled being consumed. Brokenness overwhelms. Temptation to despair seems an enemy too strong. But it's all a lie. It turns out we are not consumed. We are not devoured. The compassion of the Lord never fails us. His great love prevents us from being consumed. We are eternally rescued. Redeemed. Reconciled. Kept for that day.

While brokenness is real, the gospel—the good news—consumes brokenness. It's a wonderful paradox. It's a turn of events. Our horrible enemy never saw this coming. He's left scratching his head. He was laughing as suffering seemed to consume us, but because of God's steadfast love we are protected. Our enemy must be frustrated. The Father's compassions never fail. Never. Like manna, they are new every single morning. Wake up and face the day with this fact of faith. We are protected in His great and steadfast love. His compassions never fail. His compassions are new every morning—an endless supply. Our Father delivers on His great faithfulness.

Kim and I served in the southern part of Africa as missionaries with the International Mission Board (IMB) for more than thirteen years. God gave us the incredible privilege to serve alongside other missionaries and African believers. Later, we would be asked to move to Richmond for a new role. While there, Kim's gifts as a journalist developed into editing, compiling, and ghostwriting. She excelled and was privileged to write several books. Then empty nest and grandchildren came along. Life was sweet.

And then.

February 18, 2019. The brokenness of the world visited me, up close and personal. One day I'm planning a getaway for us, the next I'm planning her funeral. There's no denying the overwhelming sense of loss and hopelessness.

Julie Yarbrough wrote the book *Inside the Broken Heart: Grief Understanding for Widows and Widowers*. She writes, "we do not enter into grief. Grief enters into us." She is correct. To use the word in the book of Lamentations, it seems as if grief consumes you. Shock. Numbness. Confusion. Pain. Brokenness. Death. Consumed.

But, this fact of faith stands: we are not consumed.

> Brothers and sisters, we do not want you to be uninformed about those who sleep in death, so that you do not grieve like the rest of mankind, who have no hope. (1 Thessalonians 4:13)

Hope is greater than you knew.

As I have sought to mourn with hope, I have seen so clearly that the gospel narrative, the redemptive story we herald, is a story of brokenness that has met its match. We learn in Genesis that mankind fell and sin has had its way in our world. Open your eyes to our world and you see brokenness. The gospel—

the death, burial, and resurrection of Jesus—overwhelms and defeats brokenness.

Eternity is filled with hope.

This gospel-inspired, already-but-not-yet hope is inspiring and comforting. In Colossians 1:27, Paul proclaimed, "the glorious riches of this mystery, which is Christ in you, the hope of glory." We have a promised prize in eternity. One day, all will be made new. And yet, this eternal, one-day hope delivers temporal-today hope. Knowing our eternal hope, we can walk in hope in our present day. Even though we may walk through valleys. Even though we may face suffering. Walking in hope is a faith-filled decision.

Great is my hopefulness.

D. Ray Davis serves as a church strategist team leader for mobilization at the International Mission Board.

Love Your Neighbor

"Love the Lord your God with all your heart and with all your soul and with all your mind and with all your strength." The second is this: "Love your neighbor as yourself." There is no commandment greater than these.

—Mark 12:30–31

When I was just a little one, not even five years old, one of the first songs I learned was:

Jesus loves the little children,
All the children of the world;
Red and yellow, black and white,
They are precious in His sight.
Jesus loves the little children of the world.

What's really funny about this is I didn't realize I was the "red" in this song. Being Native American, my skin is brown. I wasn't taught to know people by color. Now, I know the point being made in this song is that Jesus loves all people of every language, every tribe, every ethnicity, and every race. But as a little girl, I wondered when I would ever meet someone who was red, yellow, black, or white.

I grew with a missions-minded momma and daddy who made sure we were taught the meaning, value, and importance of missions. Later, I found myself as a church WMU director and an associational WMU director first in Arizona, and then in Oklahoma. I thrived on missions.

My husband's job moved us to northern Virginia from Arizona. I didn't want to move, but I had no choice. For my first fifteen years as an elementary educator, I had only taught Native American children and among Alaska Native villages. I felt sure this was God's calling for me to teach among my own race. I was quite shocked, actually, to find myself among children of so many ethnicities. I had the most tremendous blessing of teaching children from all over the world when we lived in northern Virginia.

Many were seeing a Native American person for the first time. When we arrived, I was a substitute teacher. There were not many Native American educators in the area where we lived. One day a student stared at me all day and finally got up the nerve to ask me the question that had been on his mind all day long. His question was (and he was serious), "Where do you set up your teepee to live here?" It provided a teachable moment to share. I told him not all Native American nations are the same. We come from varied cultures and do not always practice the same way of living. It allowed me to educate him, and the rest of the students, that we live very much as they do, having assimilated to a modern way of life.

When I became a full-time teacher in the education system, many schools engaged me as a resource person to provide history about our Native American nations. I shared information about the many tribes, languages, homes, traditional values, arts, and our stories of being forced from our homeland. I found myself as a learner, too, as many students invited me to celebrations, to their homes, and even to enjoy a delicious meal at a restaurant owned by their family, serving their original delicacies.

I invited my entire class to our home one Christmas for a Christmas party, where we made ornaments, decorated cookies, took turns breaking a piñata, and enjoyed pizza and a movie. They were fascinated with our Native American pottery, baskets, and art that decorated our home, as well as our Christmas tree filled with Native American ornaments. This opened the door for two of my students to ask me what Christmas meant to me. I gladly shared with them the story of Jesus. Later, those same children asked me about Easter. I still thank God for that experience today. I loved every minute of those seven years on that mission field unlike anything I had experienced before.

If you only find yourself among your "own kind," you're missing out. I invite you to step, not just think, outside the box. Take opportunities to meet new people and befriend people very different than yourself.

I am blessed to lead the Native Praise Choir representing tribes from many Native American nations. It is awesome when we unite our choir with voices of people from many other ethnicities. I know it pleases the Father when we are one in Him. It's a great time to love your neighbor.

Augusta Smith is the executive director of The Native American LINK, Inc.

A Weight Lifted

I am the vine; you are the branches. If you remain in me
and I in you, you will bear much fruit; apart from me
you can do nothing.

—John 15:5

The moving van turned onto our street and stopped in front of an older house that had been for sale for a short period of time. Our street was in an established area of town and properties sold quickly. As household belongings were unloaded, I began planning what I would put in the "Welcome to the Neighborhood" basket. I liked to take baked goods and homemade jams to newcomers.

When my husband and I walked up to the front door several days later, loud barking and the sounds of rapid-moving paws greeted us. My husband is afraid of dogs, so I wasn't surprised to see him turn around and retreat to the sidewalk as the Great Dane barked her welcome.

We were starting our Vacation Bible School (VBS) the next Monday, so I volunteered to transport the family's two children back and forth with me and our children. Our invitation to attend church was set aside, but the mom was interested in VBS for the kids as it would enable her to unpack moving boxes in peace and quiet. Our invitation and the welcome basket was the beginning of a long relationship that lasted years.

As we got to know our new neighbors, we learned they were not involved in church nor were they certain of their relationship to Christ. Janet* had grown up with a belief system steeped in doing good works. Her husband, Jim*, had attended church as a child but never had professed faith in Jesus.

The kids loved coming to church. Many Sunday mornings we picked them up and took them with us to Sunday School. Their parents enrolled them in our church's Christian school, and we began a relationship beyond being just neighbors.

Time passed, and one day our phone rang. Janet had a question. "Would it be all right if Jim and I came to church tomorrow? Is there something for us to do while the kids attend Sunday School?"

I was so excited I don't remember exactly what I told her, but I assured her there were Bible study classes for her and Jim. She hesitated and then asked quietly, "I need to tell you something. I don't have a skirt or dress. I don't ever wear hose. Can I still come?"

"Of course, you can."

"So, it'll be OK if I wear pants? I know that's not what most women wear, but it's all I have."

As I answered yes, I hoped everyone would be welcoming of these parents whose spiritual questions were pressing in on them and they were searching for life's answers. I knew they could find hope in Jesus.

Several months went by, and our neighbors continued to participate in church activities. Early one morning, Janet called. "I did it! I accepted Jesus yesterday! I am so excited. I feel as if a huge weight has been lifted from my shoulders. All of my life I've seen God as someone who had a big chalkboard making marks of good things on one side of my name and bad things on the other. I know now that He isn't like that! His Son came to save me and stands before God in my place. What a relief! I finally have hope in my heart."

Janet confessed to me weeks later that so much had changed in her life since professing Christ. Her days were filled with purpose, and she began teaching her children about what Jesus had done for them. She laughingly said, "Even the way I cook has changed. Now I fix casseroles."

Months later I received a call from Janet telling me about Jim's decision to follow Christ. I had been ill and missed worship service. One of my greatest regrets is that I wasn't present when he walked down the aisle to share with the church that he believed in the sacrificial death of Jesus and wanted to follow Him.

When my husband asked Jim why he'd waited so long, he said, "I accepted Jesus weeks ago, but I knew if I told anyone, my co-workers would expect to see a change in my speech and behavior. I just couldn't take that step until I realized the only hope I'll ever have is in Him. I'm ready to tell others what He's done for me and that He can help them too."

Several years went by and Jim got a promotion, so another move was in the making. As he and Janet packed to move, my husband and I talked to them about finding a new church home. They promised that was at the top of their list.

We heard from them several times as they rejoiced in finding a new place to serve. The family was involved in missions, taught Bible studies, and one of their teens went on a mission's trip while the other toured the United States with a Christian music group.

Our investment in the young family's children resulted in their parents coming to Christ, the Hope of the world. Their faithfulness in learning about God's plan for their lives was seen in how they taught their children. The years of service they had in their new home demonstrated the knowledge there is indeed hope in this life and for eternity.

Hope, true lasting hope, is found in knowing Christ and learning His ways. It is this kind of hope that can revolutionize society, encompass the world, and transform lives. When we live as branches attached to the Vine, we will discover like Janet did that her works were of no value. Her spiritual security didn't lie in the good things she did. Jim's behavior wasn't changed by anything he did. Their hope lay in Christ, only Christ.

Linda Clark is a lead strategist for adult audiences at national WMU.

*names changed

Firmly Planted

Therefore, my dear brothers and sisters, stand firm. Let
nothing move you. Always give yourselves fully to the
work of the Lord, because you know that your labor in
the Lord is not in vain.

—1 Corinthians 15:58

Malika's* faith is strong and her heart beats with passion
for all peoples to know Jesus. But she lives in a 99.9
percent Muslim nation in North Africa. No one ever
shared Jesus with Malika, but the Holy Spirit drew her to Himself
when she was twelve years old. One afternoon while listening to
a brief shortwave radio broadcast from Western Europe, a man
speaking Malika's own Arabic dialect said, "Jesus is The Way, The
Truth, and The Life. There's no way to God except through Jesus."

After listening to the radio program for approximately four
months, Malika made the decision to trust Jesus and follow
Him. She had never even met a Christian. She had never seen a
Bible. Yet, she placed her hope in Christ alone.

Over the years, when Malika's faith has been challenged,
she has remembered that she stands on Christ, the solid Rock.
She knows His Word is *always* a firm place to stand. Her feet are
planted on the solid Rock and she trusts the One who is beneath
her. Malika believes that Jesus never changes. She's confident
He is the same yesterday, today, and forever (Hebrews 13:8).

Malika became my dearest friend when I moved to her
country in 2002. We met together regularly for prayer. We ate

couscous together, shopped together, laughed, and cried together. I watched her model "standing firm" when she faced trials of loss, sickness, and disappointment. She never wavered in her belief.

I have sometimes struggled with trying to stand firm in my faith. When I struggle with my faith, the evil one whispers words contrary to God's Word. Malika, by her example, has helped me choose to cast down those thoughts (2 Corinthians 10:5). Malika certainly is not perfect, but when she recognizes thoughts of fear, doubt, temptation, discouragement, or anxiety, she makes up her mind to stand firm. She chooses to guard her mind against the deception of the enemy and to think God's thoughts instead. Her hope rests in Christ alone.

Malika introduced me to Fatima*, who was on the journey to becoming a Christ-follower. She was a single woman, still living under the surveillance and authority of her father. Once a week, Fatima would make her way to the city to visit Malika. Discipleship was taking place, and I began meeting with Malika and Fatima for prayer and fellowship. What a blessing it was to observe Malika investing in Fatima's life. What a joy it was to see Fatima put her faith and trust in Jesus Christ and follow Him in believer's baptism. Baptism for a Muslim is the final cut with Islam. The church in this North African city was growing, one by one, as individuals were finding hope in Christ alone.

Then, I met Samira*, a sweet, shy young lady who had questions about the Jesus way. Malika, Fatima, and I gathered regularly with Samira for conversation and coffee.

Samira asked questions that made us all think. We all knew she would face much persecution from her family if they knew she had any doubts about Islam. She had plenty of doubts. Samira believed in her heart that Jesus died for her sins and rose from the grave after three days, but she was never able to escape the fear of being beaten or killed by her brothers. Samira stopped coming for visits. I continue to pray for her today, and

I keep trusting the One who gives peace and saves lives. I pray I will see Samira in heaven.

Ezzah* knocked on the door one afternoon as the few known believers in our North African city were gathered for worship in an old downtown building. Hesitant to open the door fully, a church member carefully concealed the inside view from this visitor as the two of them whispered, peering at each other through a small opening. Finally, the church member invited Ezzah to enter. Nobody in the room seemed to know Ezzah. We were not sure how she found our worship venue or what her intent was in coming. We did not know if she was a true seeker or a spy sent by the government.

After our worship time, I introduced myself to Ezzah and was quickly drawn to her. She appeared to be sincere about wanting to know about Jesus. We scheduled times during the next weeks to visit together. Sometimes we would meet for an hour, sometimes three to four hours. Ezzah expressed many doubts about her faith and was open to reading the Bible. She was careful to respect her own prophet but wanted to know more and more about the prophet Jesus.

One day the scales fell from her eyes and she acknowledged Jesus as more than a prophet. She prayed to Him as Holy Father. She repented of her sins and asked Jesus to take control of her heart and life. She believed in *the* one true God and His Son Jesus. The church in this North African city continued to grow, one by one, as individuals were finding hope in Christ alone.

God gives us His help and deliverance in this world. Our Lord's eternal deliverance in Jesus is sure and certain for all who believe in Him. In this time of growing change, we can rely on the power, on the love, on the earthly deliverance and on the eternal deliverance we have in Jesus.

We are called to build our lives on *the* Solid Rock of Jesus Christ and His redeeming love.

Isaiah 7:9 says, "If you do not stand firm in your faith, you will not stand at all." As the hymn says, "On Christ, the solid Rock, I stand; all other ground is sinking sand."

Debbie Moore is the executive director of Arkansas Woman's Missionary Union.

*names changed

Rest in God's Perfect Peace

You will keep in perfect peace those whose minds are
steadfast, because they trust in you. Trust in the Lord
forever, for the Lord, the Lord himself, is the Rock eternal.

—Isaiah 26:3–4

I traced my fingers along the corners of the pale yellow envelope
and took out the card. On the outside, a lovely nature scene
where butterflies and hydrangeas filled the spaces along the
borders. Along the top reflected back in big, bold letters were
the words: *"On the Loss of Your Mother."* On the inside of the
card were words that spoke of comfort, peace, and strength. As
much as I needed those words, my eyes couldn't help but focus
on the blue hydrangeas on the front cover. Hydrangeas were
her favorite after all.

Never in my wildest dreams did I think that at just thirty-two
years old I would be staring at a stack of sympathy cards on my
kitchen counter and dealing with the sudden loss of my mother.
Life is full of twists and turns, but that was a turn I didn't expect to
come so soon. It felt like my whole world had been flipped upside
down and everything I knew had changed within an instant.

As I looked over the stack of cards piled up on my kitchen
counter, God's peace overtook my heart, and I knew He was
with me. I knew He would give me strength and keep me steady
even in the hardest moments of my grief.

Maybe you are facing your own twist or turn today. Maybe you are experiencing an unexpected loss or an unwanted diagnosis, a battle with anxiety or depression, an unforeseen financial situation, or a relationship that needs mending. Or perhaps something has happened that has left you with more questions than you have answers. So many things can come along and leave us feeling like we're standing on shaky ground.

To the outside world, we shouldn't have peace about the difficulties we face, but as followers of Jesus, we know it is through His peace and His peace alone that we are able to face hard times.

In the weeks and months that followed my mother's passing, I felt the peace of God in a way I had never felt before. I felt His strength and His comfort. I could sense His closeness and I could feel His presence with me in each passing moment, especially in the moments where His love was needed the most.

When the storms of life rage around us, it is our hope in Jesus that keeps us grounded, steadfast, and immovable. We have the certainty of His peace and His peace flows in abundance to us. As hard times come our way, and we know they will come our way, we have to hold on to the hope of Jesus. We have to stand firm on the truth of God's Word and who He is.

Refuge. Rock. Comforter. Creator. Sustainer. Peace-Giver.

Anything outside of Him provides a temporary peace that will eventually fade away. When our minds are fixed on Him and we are steadfast with our trust in Him, we will find lasting peace.

Even in the midst of my grief, I can say with absolute assurance, it is well with my soul. It's not because I understand it all or because I am no longer hurting. It's not even because I can see how this all works out. It's because my soul rests in the One who changed everything.

Jesus changes everything for us.

He is the only way our mourning can be turned to dancing. Our despair can be turned into praise. And beauty brought from our ashes (see Isaiah 61).

Rest assured, even though you might feel shaky, God is never shaken. He is a refuge, a help, and a rock for us in uncertain times. Isaiah 26:3–4 tells us that the Lord himself is our eternal Rock. You can rest in the assurance of His perfect peace.

He has not left you. He has not forgotten you. He is right there with you.

I know it's hard to have hope when things around us feel like they are falling apart. Take heart, my friend. Hope is very much alive because Jesus is alive. We may not always understand what God is doing at the moment, but we can trust that what He will bring from our hardships, our grief, and our uncertainties will be good. It will be very good.

God can use the greatest trials in our lives to bring the most glory to Him and to His kingdom, and He can do a mighty work in even the most difficult of our seasons. He is still on the throne. He is still in control. He is still the only true source of lasting peace for us. The world around us may swirl with uncertainty, but God remains steadfast and faithful.

A steadfast faith doesn't come after the storms of life have passed, but often in the midst of the storms, calling us into a deeper relationship with our Creator. He is holding us. He has a plan and He can be trusted.

So hold tightly to hope. Hold tightly to His perfect peace. Hold tightly to Jesus.

Everything changes with Him. Everything.

Amanda Martinsen is a leadership development consultant and resource coordinator for WMU of North Carolina.

Be My Witnesses

But you will receive power when the Holy Spirit comes
on you; and you will be my witnesses in Jerusalem, and
in all Judea and Samaria, and to the ends of the earth.

—Acts 1:8

The event coordinator for a major church training event
in Austin, Texas, called to let me know one of their
conference leaders had to bow out at the last minute.
Lifeway Christian Resources wanted to know if I could step in
and teach four conferences that would replace the ones this
person had planned to lead. Normally this would not have been
a big deal, but the conference was less than a week away. I was
serving on a church staff in the Dallas-Fort Worth area.

I agreed to create the four training sessions to help Lifeway.
After all, I was a loyal customer and as a minister of education,
I used Lifeway's materials in all of my church's groups. I considered it an honor to help them out of a jam. But I also wanted to
reward myself for this fast work on Lifeway's behalf, so I with-
drew one hundred dollars from my savings account to play a
round of golf in the Austin area on Friday morning before we
set up for the event at the host church on Friday afternoon. It
would be my gift to me for making the trek to Austin from the
Dallas-Fort Worth area.

About halfway to Austin, I began to feel sick. A sudden
headache made it hard to concentrate, and I sneezed inces-
santly. By the time I finished my four-hour drive, I felt horrible. I pulled into the hotel parking lot thinking there's no way I

would be able to play golf early the next morning. I was right. I made it to my room, went straight to bed, and slept until mid-morning on Friday.

My symptoms weren't as severe on Friday, but I missed my opportunity to play a round of golf. I didn't feel well, and I lost my appetite. Lunch was missed, but I headed to the host church to set up. Others decided to go to dinner, but I declined. My energy was drained, and I needed to get back to my room to rest.

On the way to the hotel, though, the most amazing series of events took place.

I decided it wasn't good for me to go back to the room without eating. I went to two restaurants on my way to the hotel, but they had long wait times since it was a Friday night in Austin, Texas. I decided to forego the food, eat something from the vending machine at the hotel, and try to get a good breakfast early on Saturday.

As I pulled into the hotel parking lot, I noticed something I hadn't seen before—the restaurant next to the hotel. I parked and walked over to see if, by chance, their wait time was less than the two previous restaurants.

Unfortunately for me, it wasn't. I turned to leave the crowded foyer area, and for some reason the person at the check-in podium caught me before I left the restaurant. She may have felt pity on me. I'm sure I looked like death warmed over! In a crowded room of guests all waiting for tables, she seated me at a table for four people. And I didn't even have to wait. Miracle number one.

When my waiter came by to introduce himself, he asked about my day. I returned the favor and asked about his day, and he told me it was terrible. When I asked why, he informed me that he'd lost the money given to him by guests who'd recently left the restaurant. He thought he probably dropped the cash as he was waiting on other tables, and someone picked up the money. When I asked how much he'd lost, he said one hundred dollars.

When my food arrived and I began to eat, the Holy Spirit nudged me and said, "Give your one hundred dollars to this young man." The hair on my arms stood up. I didn't hear an audible voice, but there was no doubt God was speaking to me.

I knew I had to give this young man my golf money to replace the money he'd lost. I wrote him a long note on the back of my receipt and shared the gospel with him, gave him my name and contact information, signed it "Pastor Ken," and left it for him.

As I walked back to my hotel, I heard footsteps running up behind me. This young waiter chased me down, tears streaming down his cheeks, wanting to know why I'd gifted him the money. I told him that I freely gave him the gift, and I hoped he had received God's free gift of salvation in Christ. I made sure he knew that God loved him and that this was a gift from God to him.

I led my workshops the next day, only to discover afterwards Lifeway personnel had brought a check for me in the amount of four hundred dollars for the workshops I led. I had no clue this was part of the deal. I gave that young student one hundred dollars, and God replaced it with four hundred dollars. Miracle number two.

The next week I was surprised when this waiter called me on my cell phone. He said he had hated God for years. He blamed the church and his former pastor for breaking up his parents' marriage. He'd walked away from God and from church, never to return. He said my witness to him forever changed his perception of pastors, and more importantly, of God. Miracle number three.

Six weeks later, on a Sunday, during spring break, my family and I were on a ski trip to New Mexico, when I got a phone call from my pastor. "There's someone here who wants to talk to you."

The waiter from Austin and his entire family made the journey up to Dallas-Fort Worth to worship with me and my church family—the first time they'd been back in church since the divorce of his parents. He again told me how much the financial gift meant and how God used my witness to change his attitude about God and pastors.

Acts 1:8 tells us the early church would be Jesus' witnesses in Jerusalem, Judea, Samaria, and to the uttermost parts of the world. There are people all around us like this man who need to hear the gospel and to feel and know God's love in tangible ways. They need hope in Christ. May we be His witnesses as we go to our "uttermost parts."

Ken Braddy is a director of Sunday School and strategic network partnerships at Lifeway Christian Resources.

Hold Unswervingly to Hope

Let us hold unswervingly to the hope we profess, for
he who promised is faithful.

—Hebrews 10:23

I had heard about refugees for much of my adult life. I had met a
few along the way. But in 2014 my work with the International
Mission Board in Southeast Asia led to my regular involvement
and ministry with refugees. Most of those I have met have fled
due to persecution for religious beliefs. Some due to accepting
Christ in a location where the predominant religion opposed
belief in Christ. Others because they were a minority sect of the
predominant religion.

As I met those brothers and sisters who fled their home
countries and left all behind, one word that always stood out
to me was "hope." Their unswerving hope in Christ was what
drove them to stand firm in the faith and give up all for the
hope and joy of knowing Christ.

One family from South Asia was a dad (doctor), mom, and
three children. The first time I met them, they were in hiding
in the country they fled to as their visa had expired. They went
from a well-to-do family with little wants to living in a tiny
apartment with what they brought in suitcases with no access
to a job or school.

As they told me their story, the dad described this journey
as a refugee as "their seminary" for in losing all the things of

the world, they had learned Christ is enough and their faith had grown so deep. The children had all found a personal relationship with Christ in this journey. The nine-year-old asked if she could pray for me before I left. She prayed scriptures of praise, hope, and faith. She thanked God for the many blessings that this journey as refugees had brought to her family as they grew to know Christ in a more personal way.

The family became some of the greatest gospel proclaimers among other refugees who did not know Christ. They were unswervingly holding to the hope of Christ. They knew without a doubt that Christ was and is faithful in all times and all circumstances. I have never met any other family that lived in the hope and joy of the Lord more.

In spring 2021, I met a group of Congolese refugees in my city in Tennessee. I had heard about them for some time but had been unable to connect earlier due to various circumstances. In our first face-to-face meeting with Pastor Tibasime and four other church members, I learned the pastor had begun his service for God while living in the Congo.

Because of persecution of Christians, he and his family fled to a neighboring country where they lived in a refugee camp for several years. Many of the church members have this same experience. Some even knew each other from the camp. He shared that they had been Christians and Baptists in the refugee camp in the Congo and now wanted to join the Baptist family here. He described how they had never given up hope in Christ and His love and provision for them. "We have remained faithful to Christ, the Bible, and being Baptist." Now that they are here in America, they want to continue to be faithful in all of these.

In a testimony, Pastor Tibasime said, "First of all I thank God for everything He did for all of us. Since Mom Bonita has given us the way to be with the Baptist family, there is no problem between us. We are glad to still be able to be a Baptist church with you together as it says in Psalms 133:1. We are happy to work together as one in peace. Since we started together in

May, nothing can keep us apart. We appreciate being together working with Christ."

They know Christ is worth it all. He has always given them salvation and hope for today and the future. Their gratitude to the Father is that they can now worship and serve in peace alongside of other believers. Their greatest desire is to serve the Lord and be found faithful in Christ. They continue to share the hope of Christ with others here and regularly are baptizing new believers. We are thrilled to have our Congolese brothers and sisters as a part of our Baptist family. They remind us of how blessed we are to have hope, faith, and salvation in Christ.

I and others can tell you many stories of our refugee brothers and sisters who have held unswervingly to the hope of Christ in life's most difficult circumstances. They teach me daily that Christ is worth it because He is faithful. They challenge me to live unswervingly in the hope of Christ who is always faithful. Are you holding faithfully to the hope of Christ?

God is bringing the nations to our country so we might be encouraged by brothers and sisters of the faith who have never wavered under the most difficult of circumstances. He is bringing refugees, international students, business and professional persons, and those willing to work for a chance at a better life. Acts 17:26–27 says God determines the time and place where people live so that they might seek and find God. The internationals living in your community are not here by chance but are here because God has allowed it so they might seek, know, and grow in Christ. My challenge for you is: "Let us hold (and share) unswervingly to the hope we profess, for he who promised is faithful."

Bonita Wilson is a director of community engagement for Knox County Association of Baptists in Tennessee.

No Other Name

Salvation is found in no one else, for there is no other name under heaven given to mankind by which we must be saved.

—Acts 4:12

Being sixth-generation members of The Church of Jesus Christ of Latter-day Saints, the Wise family thought they had everything. Having both been members of the LDS Church (Mormons) for thirty-six years, Shane and Dixie believed Joseph Smith to be a prophet, believed the Book of Mormon to be God's word, and believed the current president of the LDS Church to be God's prophet for the contemporary world.

Shane grew up in the rural community of Blackfoot, Idaho, and attended Utah State University in Logan, Utah. Dixie was raised in the nearby city of Idaho Falls, Idaho, and attended Rexburg College in Rexburg, Idaho, now Brigham Young University Idaho. After they were sealed (married) in the LDS Temple in Idaho Falls, Shane and Dixie began working to build the American dream. They eventually moved to Utah, had two children, Brendon and Lauren, and worked with all their strength, not only for material wealth and prosperity through their jobs but also for spiritual wealth and prosperity through their Mormon faith. Shane and Dixie thought they had it all—a beautiful home, the typical American family, great jobs, a loving community around them, and a faith tradition that met their needs.

As the days, months, and years passed, their Latter-day Saint faith failed them. Personally, and without telling Shane, Dixie began to doubt her faith. She questioned the most fundamental doctrines of Mormonism but decided not to tell Shane because she was worried he might leave her or chastise her for doubting.

Likewise, on a business trip, Shane met two evangelical Christians who shared the gospel of the New Testament Jesus with him and he, independent of Dixie, also began to doubt his Mormon faith. In the same way as Dixie, he decided not to share his doubts with his wife because of the potential consequences.

Ultimately, the two told each other of their doubts and each was comforted by the other's doubts. The culmination of the process ended on a Sunday morning during a women's meeting at their local Latter-day Saint meeting house when Dixie was teaching. As she was teaching the women's class with the approved Latter-day Saint curriculum, Dixie simply said, "I don't believe this any longer" and walked out of the meeting.

From there, their lives spiraled downward. Because Mormonism is heavily dependent on close community among members, leaving Mormonism is not easy. Shane and Dixie left Mormonism while living in Utah, in the Salt Lake metropolitan region halfway between Salt Lake City (the administrative headquarters of Mormonism) and Provo (the cultural headquarters of Mormonism and home to Brigham Young University). Their neighborhood was nearly all Mormon. Their entire family was Mormon. All of their friends were Mormon. All of their children's friends were Mormon. Their employers were Mormon. But they left the LDS Church because they knew something was not right. And they lost everything.

As all of this was taking place, and with no knowledge of the Wise family, a church in Herriman, Utah, very close to Shane and Dixie's home, was preparing for a block party in an attempt to share the gospel with their surrounding neighborhood. People from the church canvased the neighborhood and handed out invitations to people as they walked around. Providentially, one of the church members met Dixie at a park and handed her an invitation. She reluctantly accepted.

As the day for the block party approached, Shane and Dixie wrestled with whether or not they should attend. The block party was scheduled for Saturday, July 18—Dixie's birthday. Usually, the Wise family went out for a nice meal to celebrate birthdays, but this particular birthday, Dixie was not in the proper emotional place to enjoy a night out because of everything the family lost due to their leaving Mormonism. She hesitantly told Shane they would just go to the block party and celebrate her birthday with a hotdog or hamburger. Shane and Dixie told their children to enjoy the party and, as the children ran off to play, Shane and Dixie found a shade tree to sit under, completely separated from the activity of the block party.

A member of the church, Vicki, saw Shane and Dixie sitting under the tree and approached them to offer a greeting and share the gospel. After a few minutes of conversation with Shane and Dixie, Vicki came to get me and told me she had met a couple who had some questions about Mormonism. I walked over, met Shane and Dixie, and said, "I hear you have some questions."

With deep hurt in her eyes and anger in her voice, Dixie looked at me. "I want to know about the priesthood and temples. Go."

I answered their questions, shared the gospel with them, and made sure they understood, "Salvation is found in no one else, for there is no other name under heaven given to mankind by which we must be saved" (Acts 4:12).

They both placed their faith in Christ and, later that evening, shared the same gospel with Brendon and Lauren, and their two children placed their faith in Christ. On July 18, Dixie's physical and spiritual birthday, the eternal destiny of Shane, Dixie, Brendon, and Lauren Wise was permanently changed from death to life. Their souls were regenerated because of the power of the Holy Spirit through the proclaimed word of Christ. They found hope in Christ because there is no other name through which hope can be found.

Jesus is indeed the only place to find hope. Peter's bold declaration in Acts 4:12 makes this clear and leaves no doubt.

Although some may believe hope can be found through Joseph Smith (Mormonism), Muhammad (Islam), Ellen White (Seventh-Day Adventism), Siddhartha Gautama (Buddhism), L. Ron Hubbard (Scientology), or their own human works, true hope cannot be found in any other name than the name of Jesus Christ, the Son of God and second person in the Trinity. May each of us be ministers of reconciliation (2 Corinthians 5:18) and share the hope of Christ with each person the Lord puts in our path. Indeed, "Salvation is found in no one else, for there is no other name under heaven given to mankind by which we must be saved."

Travis Kerns is an associational mission strategist at Three Rivers Baptist Association in South Carolina.

Journey into One

I have been crucified with Christ and I no longer live,
but Christ lives in me. The life I now live in the body, I
live by faith in the Son of God, who loved me and gave
himself for me.

—Galatians 2:20

When God directed me to quit my job to become a writer, I laughed. I was a poor English student so why would God call me to a task beyond my intelligence? After two years of fighting, I finally submitted to God's call on my life. With pen in hand and a yellow notepad, I began to write poetry, then short stories, and finally my first book. I assumed my writing would be a source of income, but God was going to use my writing to bring me into a closer relationship with Him.

Soon I collected enough stories to publish my first book. When the books were printed, I planned a book tour to introduce myself as a writer and sell books. I had no idea how to plan such a feat, but God was working His plan. I traveled from New Orleans to Boston, making stops along the way with friends to share stories and sell books. As I prepared for the trip, God told me to take no money and call the trip "JOURNEY INTO ONE." I had no idea what that meant, but I was willing to follow God's plan. I was so excited to share my new ministry, but something else was stirring in my spirit that had nothing to do with book sales.

For twenty-five days traveling thousands of miles, I journeyed alone with God. He rode with me and talked with me as I traveled, revealing His plan for a new ministry. Traveling many miles through the prettiest scenes, God showed me the ugliness of my soul. Tears fell down my face as I released those things that hindered me from proclaiming God's truth. I had a long way to go before the sweetness of Jesus flowed through my heart.

Every stop showed more of the people of God. I saw hearts rather than race, color, or religion. God created everybody in His image with the intent that we learn to live together as family. I recognized the uniqueness of people who were creations of God who commanded unity as a family. I spent time with so many different people, seeing Jesus everywhere I went. I was looking through the eyes of God rather than through the eyes of my own ethnicity.

Being born into an interracial family, I never had a problem relating to other races. Yet in my heart, I knew that racism caused a great division among God's people. I was blessed that God had given me a rich heritage of greatness. I was the proud great-granddaughter of a slave, the granddaughter of a sharecropper, and the daughter of a janitor who worked hard so that I could experience the freedom to be what God wanted me to be. Some African Americans often said I had a pseudo-superiority complex. I never quite understood what that meant, but I knew I was different from most. I was strong willed with a mind of my own and that attitude got me in trouble with people who sought pleasure in trying to control me.

God's Word is filled with story after story of God bringing different people together. During His time on earth, Jesus gave the only solution for racial reconciliation. I made an interesting discovery that it's only the love of God that will ever make us one. Oneness does not mean sameness. I hate being stereotyped. I love my uniqueness. Like the example of Paul, I can still be me, but my heart opens the door so that others can fall in love with the Jesus they see in me. I don't feel agreeing to disagree is a Christian response to developing godly relationships. Jesus never agreed to disagree with anyone. Love must be the thread that joins us together as family. It's that same love that looks beyond faults to see the need for a relationship with Christ.

Again, I was in front of that mirror displaying more of my ugliness to God. I heard Him say to my spirit, "Friends don't come in colors." That message forever changed my racist attitude. I learned to embrace differences so we can learn to live as children of God. I had nothing to prove to white folk and they owed me nothing, but both of us needed to understand that God wanted to use us to show Jesus to the world. It is only through being honest and transparent that we will ever learn to enjoy the abundant life God gives to all His children. I began to embrace the differences of my friends so we might show the world how to live as family.

Returning home from my journey into one, I emerged from God's cocoon with my new wings ready to fly. People thought I found a new boyfriend, but I found something better, intimacy with God.

Gwen Williams, Ms. Chocolate, is a storyteller and author in Picayune, Mississippi.

I Am in Their Midst

For where two or three gather in my name,
there am I with them.

—Matthew 18:20

Several years ago, my wife, Carol, and I boarded a plane at the Birmingham-Shuttlesworth Airport in Alabama and flew to Taipei, Taiwan, to adopt our daughter Lauren. Our hearts were filled with hopeful anticipation. She would be our first child after almost nine years of marriage. After landing, we discovered that our host didn't show up, and we could not speak Mandarin.

Carol glanced across the information desk and noticed the logo of our hotel. She pointed it out to a taxi driver, and we were on our way. The following day, we were greeted in the hotel lobby by social workers who placed our daughter into our arms. This fragile, beautiful child felt as if she weighed thousands of pounds. I had never felt the weight of responsibility of being a father. My joy was inexpressible.

Shock, Delight, and Amazement

In a few days, we boarded the plane for home. Family, friends, and the church I pastored waited anxiously to meet our daughter. I buckled in and prepared to hold our amazing, squalling infant for the seventeen-hour flight. The flight attendant handed me a bag of pretzels, and I snacked away.

My wife leaned over and calmly whispered to me, "I think I am expecting."

I coughed and choked on the pretzels as the news sank in. The tiny airline-sized can of soda did little to wash down my shock, delight, and amazement. "Could it be that God gave us this child by adoption and had planned all along to bless us with a birth child?" I asked.

Carol's doctor's visit after our return home verified her suspicions were fact. Eight months went by. I was sitting in my study preparing a message on the faithfulness of God, and the phone rang. Carol was hysterical. "The doctor says we have to go to the hospital now!" After the pregnancy went to full term, our precious, red-haired daughter Julianne was stillborn.

Shattered Hope

The grief that set in was unbearable. My father had to make the funeral arrangements for our stillborn daughter. I was surprised by the flood of emotions overwhelming me. I prayed, "God, I thought you were blessing us with an adopted daughter and a birth child. This was your plan after nine years of waiting. Why did you take our daughter from us? How can I comfort and support my wife? I am hurting too, Lord. I feel so guilty for mourning this child because you have given us another precious child from the other side of the world. Help me, Lord." We clung to the promise of 2 Corinthians 4:17: "For our light and momentary troubles are achieving for us an eternal glory that far outweighs them all."

Simultaneously, we were new parents, and we were suffering the loss of a baby. Our family needed the support of our church more than ever. I discovered that as the church's pastor, I needed the help and support of my church family. Frankly, that was a harsh realization for me.

I was a driven, self-sufficient leader. The church was launching a second campus and expanding our ministries. I was arrogant and proud, thinking I always had to be the strong luminary—

giving care but seldom receiving support. The staff had to push through the wall of pride I built to minister to my family and me. In the presence of the team, one friend put his arm around my shoulders and said softly, "Pastors are just people too." His words lifted a burden. However, a sting of conviction flowed into my heart as I contemplated his statement.

Jesus in Our Midst

This friend's encouragement was a well-spoken, gentle word of correction. "Pastors are *just* people too." In the presence of my staff team, this mature Christ-follower brought the loving admonishment of the church to bear upon my arrogance, chiseling away the pride. It dawned upon me that my self-sufficiency had kept me from accepting the support I needed from Jesus and the church. That moment was a fulfillment of Jesus' promise in the Gospel of Matthew: "For where two or three gather in my name, there am I with them" (Matthew 18:20). Jesus was in our midst as this friend shared grace and truth when I needed them both.

With a renewed authenticity and vulnerability in my life, Jesus began to bring emotional healing to my pain. Jesus and His people shepherded me through one of my darkest seasons. The church I served displayed grace when the quality of my sermons dropped due to my mental fatigue. Faithful deacons stepped up financially to cover the cost of my wife's medical exams and to pay for our child's funeral expenses. Later, on my tenth anniversary as the church's pastor, the leadership council of my church provided me with a much-needed sabbatical so I could be refreshed and revived in the Lord's work. Jesus was in our midst, providing every need. There is hope in Christ.

We are not omnicompetent or omnipotent. We need Jesus and His church in our midst to encourage or correct us. Only the presence of Jesus can guide us through the painful consequences of a fallen world. If we humbly invite Jesus and the church into our lives, we can receive divine strength to sustain us in our uncertainty. Jesus will make our burdens lighter and give us wisdom for the journey. So likewise, we carry the burdens of our brothers and sisters and fulfill our mission as ambassadors of Jesus (Galatians 6:2).

Take a moment right now and recognize the presence of Jesus in your midst. Perhaps you need the wisdom of the church to speak into your life and provide redirection and clarity (see Matthew 18:15). Imagine the joy you could experience today if you lived in recognition of the presence of Jesus.

Chris Crain is the executive director of Birmingham Metro Baptist Association.

Hope at Hartland Place Apartments

But God demonstrates his own love for us in this: While
we were still sinners, Christ died for us.

—Romans 5:8

The hope we have in Christ comes from the reality that God made the first move. While we were rebellious, unrighteous, and messed up, our God took the first step by sending His Son to live among us. Jesus demonstrated the gracious love of God for while we were still sinners, He shed His blood on the cross for us.

What happens when three Christian women genuinely believe Romans 5:8 and seek to live it out? Teresa, Michelle, and Sylicia started praying, seeking God, and stepping out in faith.

God gave each woman a heart's desire to find a multifamily housing community in Jackson, Tennessee, where no church was currently serving. While investigating a large mobile home park for a possible summer Vacation Bible School (VBS), they discovered a few churches were already serving there. They knew they must move on and seek God's direction for the right place.

The women approached several apartment managers, but found closed doors to their desire to conduct a summer VBS. They kept hoping, praying, and seeking.

Then one day they discovered a large apartment complex with a manager who was thrilled to hear about the possibility of these ladies and members of West Jackson Baptist Church wanting to conduct a summer VBS for his residents. He was so welcoming and promised his personal help and the approval of the owners.

As they left the manager's office, all three women looked at each other. "This is it. This is where God has been leading us." Now they had to find volunteers, work out a date for the summer VBS, find teaching materials, purchase craft supplies, buy snacks and drinks, and a host of other things. They also wanted to give every child a Bible. They would later discover that it would be the first Bible for most of the children.

Some resistance was expressed by a few church members because the apartment facility was in a high-crime area. The three women proceeded and set a date. One hundred and three children heard about Jesus that week and more than one hundred volunteers helped at different times. Two young boys prayed to receive Jesus as Savior that week and all the workers were filled with joy and praised God. A ladies' Bible study was also started with two women from church serving as teachers.

Many thought it was a wonderful week and said, "Let's do it again next year!"

The three women—Teresa, Michelle, and Sylicia—sensed the Lord leading them to do something on a weekly basis.

The apartment manager offered a free apartment to be used. That October, the first Hartland Place Apartment Bible Study began with seventeen children, two women, and twelve volunteers. A Christmas celebration was held in the community center with eight families represented and twenty children. The kids acted out the nativity scene and many gifts were poured out on the children and families. A meal was shared and much love could be felt that night. When the first year ended, attendance to the Monday night Bible study had reached sixty kids enrolled. Four children and two women had accepted Jesus. The apartment manager, his wife, and daughter were baptized at West Jackson Baptist Church.

The next May, two young Hartland boys were baptized in an open-air worship service at Hartland Place. The church purchased a large fiberglass stock tank for watering livestock, and it was a joyful time of worship and praise as many residents, church members, and kids gathered to sing and worship as these two followed the Lord in believers' baptism by immersion. The community was invited to a cookout.

What the Lord started has continued, and it has expanded in scope and impact.

Meals are provided every Monday night for the kids. The church helps with donations for beds, sofas, tables, chairs, lamps, clothing, and food. Volunteers move furniture and host free rummage sales.

A special Christmas program takes place each year as every child is given three gifts and a bag of groceries for their family. The children participate in a program that teaches the true meaning of Christmas.

Backpacks filled with school supplies are given each year to kids as school starts. Sensing the need to help kids in their studies, a tutoring class was started on Wednesday nights to help children with their homework. A library was started so children could check out books and Christian-based movies.

Eighth graders and up go on a summer adventure and spend three days at a camp with lakes, fishing, hiking, games, campfires, Bible studies, and worship. It has been a time of building relationships and seeing children and youth coming to faith in Jesus.

Latarious was one the first young men baptized through Hartland ministry. He continued attending through high school. He is now working as a young adult and doing well in life. Before her death, Teresa (one of the three original women) got her husband Mark involved in teaching boys, and Latarious was a young man who Mark grew close to. "Latarious was a kind of a natural leader. He regularly invited other friends," reflected Mark.

Mark and Latarious recruited other boys to form a basketball team to play in the church league. The team stayed together through high school as Mark worked with them and invited them to his home for several pool parties and special outings.

Hartland Community Church started in the summer of 2015 by former international missionaries and members of West Jackson Baptist Church. They meet in the Community Center each Sunday.

So many other people could have been named as faithful servants of this ongoing ministry. They would all wish to give God all the glory for the things He has done as this ministry goes into its fifteenth year of sharing the hope and the gospel of Jesus Christ.

Ron F. Hale is retired after forty years of ministry as a pastor, church starter strategist, director of missions, and state evangelism director.

Citizenship Brings Hope

If anyone speaks, they should do so as one who speaks
the very words of God. If anyone serves, they should do
so with the strength God provides, so that in all things
God may be praised through Jesus Christ. To him be
the glory and the power for ever and ever. Amen.

—1 Peter 4:11

M any people have impacted my life as I've walked shoulder to shoulder with them. When my husband and I started working with Foundations of Faith Dairy Ministry in Portales, New Mexico, I had the honor of walking shoulder to shoulder with A. B. Najera. His name was Abundio, but everyone called him "A. B." He was down-to-earth, kind, caring, and always ready to share the hope he had found in Christ.

He exemplified 1 Peter 4:11. He spoke the very words of God and served with a strength that could only come from God. He did all of this not for his own glory, but so God would be praised by more and more people.

A. B. Najera is a name many have never heard, but there is a group of men and women all over eastern New Mexico and West Texas who know the name well. Most of us will never run into this group of people who came to love A. B., but you probably enjoy their work every day with your bowl of cereal. These men and women work at dairies. They spend their days doing the hard (and dirty) work that many would not enjoy. Milking cows, taking care of new calves, putting out feed, working on equipment, and doctoring sick animals are not jobs most of us are familiar with. These dairy workers often work twelve-hour shifts six or seven days a week. Many of them have moved from other countries to escape a very poor lifestyle that few of us can even comprehend. And most do not speak English.

This was all very familiar to A. B. He began working as a delivery boy in Mexico when he was just nine years old after the death of his father. He later worked as a carpenter's assistant and then as a cook for a mining company. During this time, he married the love of his life, whom he had known since they were just seven years old.

After he and Sandra married, he became a welder for the mining company and worked as a welder and mechanic for the next thirty years in Mexico and then in the United States after they immigrated in 1986. He brought his family (including his mother-in-law and four children) to the United States to provide a better life for them.

Immigration to the United States brought two important citizenships. A. B. became a US citizen but he also learned about heavenly citizenship and became a Christian, beginning his new life following Christ. Still working as a welder and mechanic, he began pastoring Spanish-speaking churches in Texas and later moved to New Mexico. He never spent much time in an office. Instead, he chose to work with his hands and use the skills God had given him as a way to share the hope of that heavenly citizenship.

When he became a chaplain for Foundations of Faith, A. B. worked with Arturo Villa, another chaplain. Each week they would visit around forty dairies. They walked through the "muck" to share Jesus with a group of people whom others wouldn't want to spend time with. That "dairy smell" is not one you quickly wash off or forget. A. B. didn't care. His only mission was making sure men and women knew about Jesus.

The chaplains visited dairies handing out soda and bottles of water as a way to start relationships with the Spanish-speaking workers. They would then plan Bible studies at the dairies. Many of the younger workers thought of A. B. as a father. They looked up to him.

A. B. was the volunteer pastor for a small Spanish-speaking congregation, but I never heard him preach in a church. I did hear him preach many times standing outside a dairy with cows all around. He shared that the only hope worth finding in this world is found in Jesus. While he worked with the dairy ministry, he helped lead hundreds of dairy workers to Christ.

The COVID-19 pandemic changed a number of things about the ministry, but A. B. was determined to serve with the strength God provides. He began recording short daily devotions that he would share with dairy workers, friends, and family. He contracted COVID and was very sick. Even while sick, he recorded and posted devotions on social media. As soon as things began to open up, A. B. and Arturo were back visiting the dairy workers.

Starting Bible studies again was a little slow. They visited the workers and asked how they could pray for them. At one particular dairy visit, they talked to a manager and received permission to begin Bible study. As they were talking with workers in the milk room that same day, the workers asked when they could start Bible study. The chaplains told them they could schedule one for the next week. "No," the workers said. "We need to hear about God today. Let us hook the cows up to the milking machines and then you will have ten minutes to tell us about God."

While the workers got the cows ready to milk, A. B. got his Bible. He had ten minutes to share the hope that is found in a relationship with Jesus. And share he did. That ten-minute, spur-of-the-moment Bible study ended with five dairy workers finding hope in Christ as their Lord and Savior.

A. B.'s favorite Scripture was Philippians 4:13: "I can do all this through him who gives me strength." He could quote it to you in English, but he preferred his heart language of Spanish, "Todo lo puedo en Cristo que me fortalece." He knew the only way to accomplish what God has planned for each of us is through the One who gives us strength.

In March 2021, A. B. died in a car accident on his way home from church. We are heartbroken that he is no longer with us, but because A. B. Najera spoke the very words of God and served with the strength God provided, heaven has more citizens.

Melissa Lamb is the executive director of New Mexico Woman's Missionary Union.

An External Manifestation of Hope

> Do not conform to the pattern of this world, but be transformed by the renewing of your mind. Then you will be able to test and approve what God's will is—his good, pleasing and perfect will.
>
> —Romans 12:2

As a biblical counselor, I am privileged to have a front row seat to witness the amazing Holy Spirit transformation occurring in the lives of many women. Let me share one story.

Watching a new counselee pull into a parking space and get out of her car, I noticed how slowly and deliberately she moved as she walked around her car to retrieve her purse, Bible, and tote bag. With her head hung low and her shoulders slumping, she headed to the church entrance where I was waiting. It looked as if the weight of the entire universe was on her shoulders.

My greeting was met with an almost apologetic, "I'm Z*."

On her completed forms, she marked that she was a Christ-follower, read her Bible, and attended church regularly. She gave a credible testimony of her salvation experience.

Z's heartrending story that began to unfold about her younger life was horrific and filled with egregious abuse—spiritual, emotional, mental, and physical.

I asked, "Where was God when you experienced all of that horrible, abusive treatment?"

She shook her head. "I don't know," she said, looking directly into my eyes for the first time.

Z was tethered to her past and had learned to blame everything that went wrong and all the hurts she experienced in her life on things that happened in her past. All of her thoughts, emotions, and actions sprang forth from her deep-seated and now very comfortable identity as a victim.

We started with the gospel and talked about how the gospel leads us to salvation and how it also reminds and encourages Christ-followers to remain obedient and faithful in our walk with Christ.

Working through devotional journaling exercises helped her interact with the biblical truths she read and studied throughout each week and gave us excellent springboards to discuss who God is and what He says. We talked about the holiness and sovereignty of God, mankind's sinfulness, the finished work of Christ on the cross that atoned for our sins, how to resist temptation, and how to ask forgiveness for the sins we commit.

I continually stressed that God would help her look at those painful memories, deal with them biblically, and enable her to walk in the hope and freedom that comes through an unhindered, vital relationship with Christ.

Looking at her past, we discussed God's presence, protection, enablement, grace, and mercy. She was really soaking in all that she was learning and her faith in Christ was increasing exponentially.

I taught Ephesians 2:1–10 and made certain she understood that as a Christ-follower she no longer has to live without Christ as those who are described in verses 1 through 3. Before Christ we were dead in our trespasses and sins, disobedient children following the desires of our heart, and deserving of God's wrath. We were lost without any hope.

I explained that we often assess our situation as dire or hopeless and we wrongly convince ourselves that we are so sinful that God could not possibly love us. Then, we read one of many glorious phrases in Scripture—*But God*—and EVERYTHING changes.

As we proceeded reading verses 4 through 10, we were reminded that God is rich in mercy. We don't get what we deserve. Eternal death is what we deserve because of our sin against holy God. God is love, and He directs His great love toward us. Although we deserve punishment and eternal death, *God made us alive together with Christ* as He redeemed us and made us His children.

In time, Z began sitting up straight in her chair. Her shoulders weren't slumping. She not only looked at me when she spoke, she smiled.

I shared with Z a question my friend Earle would ask. "Are you wearing your grave clothes? Or are you wearing your grace clothes?" He was asking, "Are you living as if you are still dead in your trespasses and sins, or are you living as a new creation in Christ Jesus whose hope is in Him alone?"

I asked, "What do you think has made the change I see in you?"

"Jesus was right there with me. I gave up hope, resigning myself to be a victim for the rest of my life," she said, confidently. "I chose to let the past define me. I am a child of the sovereign God who is always with me. He helps me walk through any situation—past, present, and future—with hope and confidence that He is in control. He is helping me look at my past, through the lens of His mercy, grace, love, and kindness. He has helped me to cut those ties and emotions that tethered me to my past."

I shouted, "Whoopee! Thank you, Jesus!"

Z was not the same—inside nor outside—because of God's mercy and grace as she learned to trust and hope in Him. Because of the transforming work of the Holy Spirit in her life, she knows and trusts Jesus as the only real source of hope.

Z learned that regardless of what happened to her in the past and what she was back then, Christ saved her from her hopelessness and deadness, to make her alive in Him by His marvelous work of grace. He made her a new creation ready to serve Him! And that, my friend, is a new beginning indeed.

The God of hope transformed Z's heart, thus changing her outward appearance. Regardless of what is in your past or present, or what the future holds, He can certainly transform your life as you spend time with Him in prayer, in His Word, obeying His Word, with renewed hope in God.

Shirley Crowder is a Christian author and speaker in Birmingham, Alabama.

*name changed

The Hope of the Global Church

May the God of hope fill you with all joy and peace as
you trust in him, so that you may overflow with hope
by the power of the Holy Spirit.

—Romans 15:13

In tumultuous times, we can easily lose hope. We discover hope can become more slippery and fragile than we thought, especially if we inadvertently placed our hope in anything other than God and His Word. Though tempted to find our hope in people, comfort, money, platforms, politics, or even ourselves, we find our hope truly blossoms when it is firmly located in God's story. His story, we discover, is often much more grandiose than we realize. When we feel despair in our current situation, when we wring our hands and wonder what God is doing, we must remember that God, the God of hope, is moving in ways we sometimes cannot even fathom. He is building His church, even when we cannot see it.

My life took an unexpected turn in 2014, when, after much prayer and deliberation, I applied for a PhD. For years, I wanted to be on the frontlines of missions, going to the places where no one had ever heard the name of Jesus. My decision to get my PhD felt like a monumental change. Instead of packing two suitcases to move to the other side of the globe, I packed up a car and drove across the United States. Instead of experiencing days filled with the excitement of new people and new places, my new world often included a familiar routine, a stack of books, and a computer. To be honest, I knew this was my next step, but I had no idea why. The campus I frequented seemed so far from the mission field for which I had prepared.

I had no idea God would place me in a unique role that gave me a unique vantage point of hope. While finishing my PhD, I worked in Global Theological Initiatives at Southeastern Baptist Seminary. We train leaders around the world. We work with national seminaries or Bible colleges, missions sending agencies, and Baptist conventions. In this job, I came face-to-face with the reality of the global church.

From my office in North Carolina, I work with people from the nations. My co-workers include an Iranian refugee who is now preparing theological education opportunities for the fastest-growing church in the Muslim world, a Cuban American who loves the New Testament and Greek and trains hundreds of Spanish-speakers, a Korean who has a heart for raising up leaders who speak the diverse languages across Southeast Asia, and many others. I have witnessed God raise up men and women from the nations with a desire to train the nations.

I have also interacted with leaders around the globe who passionately love Jesus and His mission. For example, I assisted an educational cohort made up of many of the executive staff of two mission boards in Brazil. I helped a cohort of students in Eastern Europe comprised of Bible school teachers from around the area. I celebrated with Ugandans, Kenyans, Rwandans, and others as they graduated with a theological master's degree and prepared for ministries all over East Africa. I know faces and names of Christians in Africa, Asia, Latin America, and Europe who strive to equip their own people for God's mission.

From my unique vantage point, I can tell you something that should bring you hope: God is on the move. In Matthew 16:18, Christ promised to build His church and asserts that the gates of Hades will not overcome it. Jesus keeps His promises. He is building His church in hard places around the world.

When we are tempted to despair about the church in North America, we can turn our eyes to the blossoming churches around the world. We can recognize we have brothers and sisters across the globe who are worshipping God, training leaders, and sending missionaries. And many of these Christians are praying for the church in North America. In other words, they are praying for us.

When Paul writes to the church in Rome, he encourages them, saying, "May the God of hope fill you with all joy and peace as you trust in him, so that you may overflow with hope by the power of the Holy Spirit."

It has always struck me that when Paul writes to the church in Rome, he encourages a church he didn't plant and probably did not even know. Yet he wrote this theological treatise for them, explaining the intricacies of the gospel and the applications of such good news for their lives.

In Romans 15, Paul describes God's mercy to the nations, quoting various passages from the Old Testament that foretold their engrafting into God's family. And then he explodes with this joyful encouragement that links their joy, peace, and hope to their trust in the God of hope. Paul points to the biblical picture of a God who loves the nations to call the church in Rome to hope.

Just like the church in Rome, we can have joyful, peaceful hope because we serve a God whose love reaches to the farthest ends of the earth. The reality of the global church should encourage us. It is a visible reminder we can trust the God of the nations and praise the One who keeps His promises.

The church of God is growing. Some days we can see growth as we watch people descend into the water on a baptism Sunday or celebrate a new church plant. Other times, the growth is hidden, spreading like roots of a tree, often unseen, winding and inching along and exploding to the surface periodically. We may never hear what God is doing in the little villages, the unexpected corners of a megacity, or the places most hostile to His gospel, but we can find hope because God is moving.

He builds His church around the world, calling people from different languages, tribes, nations, and tongues to worship Him. And in knowing and trusting Him to build His church, we can find joy, peace, and hope.

Anna Daub is the director of special projects and partnerships and global theological initiatives at Southeastern Baptist Theological Seminary.

Trust Is a Word of Hope

Trust in the LORD with all your heart and lean not on
your own understanding;
in all your ways submit to him, and he will make your
paths straight.

—Proverbs 3:5–6

I was a pastor's wife and a prodigal. It started in another church where my husband and I were a ministry team. He preached, and I handled the music. Although our church was small, we had some people with tremendous talent and training. We did some nice things musically.

Each year our Baptist association had a choir festival. There was nothing I liked better than taking "my" choir and being the best there. We were all small churches in that association and most of the churches had people with little formal training as their music leaders. I, however, had a master's degree in church music, and we didn't do Stamps-Baxter gospel music. Pride was a major problem in my life at the time.

At our next church, I did not have a place on the team. The church had a music director and organist who had worked together for a number of years. They were comfortable with each other and not particularly interested in changing the team even though I felt that my training would be a great help. However, no one was going to budge and neither was God.

How I prayed for God to give me "my" position as music director. I cried often over the situation and hated to attend services. I prayed and waited for God to answer. He was silent.

I found many things to do such as a part-time job in our associational office, service as associational WMU director, and involvement in nursing home ministry, yet I was not happy. Eventually, I began counseling and at the same time was asked to teach an adult Sunday School class. As a pastor's wife in small churches, I had taught every age group except adults. But I agreed to teach the class.

I learned quickly that God's timing is always perfect. The first lesson was on anger. I began class by saying, "Well, folks, I can't teach this lesson very well. I have started counseling this week because I am a very angry person. But we'll talk about it." One of the class members gave me a gift that day when she said, "Well, maybe this is the place you can be yourself and be accepted." The Bible came alive in my life in a new way and I learned that it *is* relevant to the problems we face.

I taught that class for the next three years. Intense Bible study began to have an impact on me. The Christian counselor helped me talk through issues over a six-month period. It all came together as I drove home from work one day and prayed out loud in my car, "God, I don't know what you're doing in my life, but whatever it is, it's OK."

When I got home that day, the phone was ringing. Our state WMU director was calling to ask me to be part of a women's team going to Rwanda, Africa. I was astounded. Over the next few weeks God provided what was needed, and I prepared to make a life-changing journey.

Sometime later, I read the story of the prodigal son (Luke 15:11–32) and saw myself in that story for the first time. I had been in the far country of depression and anger, but when I determined to go home to God, it seemed as if God summoned angels by saying, "She is coming home. Get a special party ready." What a party it was as I traveled overseas on my first international missions trip with five other women. All I could do was marvel at what God had done in my life.

In the ensuing years, I have reflected many times on the prayer I prayed aloud in my car. It was my moment of trusting in the Lord with all my heart and not depending on what I could understand. I count that moment as second only to my salvation experience as of utmost importance in my life spiritually. Out of that prayer, God changed my entire direction and I have found the promise of these verses to be true.

Trusting God with all your heart brings hope, whereas reliance on your own understanding is usually hopeless in the face of difficult circumstances. Submitting to God's will is key to finding your way as He "makes your paths straight," or as the KJV says, "He shall direct thy paths."

After the trip to Rwanda and my attitude change, God opened doors I could never have imagined. I was invited to join the South Carolina WMU staff and later asked to lead Kentucky WMU. I have been on mission trips to Rwanda, Kyrgyzstan, Romania, Poland, Brazil, Tanzania, Malawi, South Korea, Indonesia, South Africa, Puerto Rico, a country in North Africa (not named for security), and Israel. God has allowed me to write, teach, and assist the work of WMU in numerous ways.

Yet, the music thing is still a struggle at times. I know that just as Moses was not allowed to enter the promised land because of his sin at Meribah (Numbers 20), God has disciplined me in closing the door of music leadership. We have served in other churches and I still do not lead music. But one thing happened at my retirement that told me God was nevertheless pleased. Out of the blue, our church choir director invited me to conduct my favorite anthem, "And the Father Will Dance" by Mark Hayes.

At first, I said no, fearing I would cry all the way through it. Somehow, I knew God was saying, "I know the struggle this has been for you and I want you to know that I am pleased." Trust is indeed a word of hope!

Joy Bolton is a retired state WMU executive director and currently serves as the volunteer international WMU coordinator for national WMU.

The Power of Problems

Consider it pure joy, my brothers and sisters, whenever
you face trials of many kinds, because you know that
the testing of your faith produces perseverance. Let
perseverance finish its work so that you may be mature
and complete, not lacking anything.

—James 1:2–4

"The one thing I lack is more problems," said no one ever!
Sleep, time, peace and quiet, friends, romance, education,
respect, health are all more likely to fill in the spot of the
empty blank that will make life complete, or at least better.

In the South Bronx where I live and work, there is an
epidemic of addiction made evident by the zombie-like men
and women who wander the street. Each are looking for the one
thing their brains have been chemically rewired to constantly
lack: their next hit of heroin. Those of us who try to help these
homeless nomads normally start by providing food, water,
clothes, or shelter. All these things are lacking from a vagrant's
life and would seemingly make their life better. However, those
of us who have all our necessities know these things alone don't
offer hope and make life complete.

As I have mentored kids who have become teenagers, and
teenagers who have become young adults, my most frequent
request in prayer for these now twentysomethings is stability. It
often seems like the one thing they lack is steady ground to find
their footing in life. The sidewalks lining Cypress Avenue quake
from problems with family, boyfriends, girlfriends, unhealthy

relationships, landlords, the opps (the street word for enemy), law enforcement, and courts.

I heard the plea of a shaking soul one evening on the stoop of my building as I talked with a young man who used to be in our afterschool program. With tears in his eyes, he said, "I never knew life would be this hard. I'm stuck. I can't get unstuck because everything has a cost. I need more money."

Many would agree with this young man. Money often seems to be what we lack, even for those of us who have all we need— it never seems to be enough. Many people's daily feelings are governed by a mathematical calculation. They count their problems, then count their money. If the problems outnumber the dollars, they worry and scurry. If the dollars outnumber the problems, they may feel better, but life still feels incomplete.

One time Jesus was talking to a man who had all the money he needed, yet he knew he was still lacking. He asked Jesus, "What must I do to inherit eternal life?" (Mark 10:17). Jesus ultimately answered his question by saying, "One thing you lack . . . Go, sell everything you have and give to the poor, and you will have treasure in heaven. Then come, follow me" (Mark 10:21).

This man didn't lack money. Neither did he lack religion; after all, he spent his entire life obeying God's law (Mark 10:20). What did he lack? He lacked problems only God could solve!

If he gave his money to the poor—all of it—his life would certainly have a few more problems. Solutions to these problems would no longer rest in his sufficiency or ability. He would also learn, as anyone who ministers to the poor learns, that money alone doesn't solve the problems in the world.

Although his charity would help *some* of the poor with *some* of their problems, it wouldn't solve *all* the problems of *all* the poor. It wouldn't even solve *all* the problems for *one* person. After all, this man was still plagued by a feeling of lack that neither the salve of money nor self-righteousness could heal.

In the Bronx, every day I am bombarded with problems only God can solve. Hardly a day goes by without my utterance, "Lord, help!" Occasionally, others join me in that prayer.

They don't always express it with those exact words, but it is prayed, nonetheless.

It was expressed by a street rapper from our block who is fighting several cases in court. His plea came in the form of a heartfelt hug after I spent time helping him with the court process and said a prayer for him.

Another time I saw this prayer outside a pizza shop in the tears of a young adult. This forlorn and sentimental young man had been fighting suicidal thoughts after he found out his girlfriend cheated on him. After spending an hour talking in the pizza shop, we were about to go our separate ways when he embraced me. I prayed for him, and he wept in my arms.

Then there's the time I heard it in the yearnings of a young man who wanted to help his struggling brother and friends. I had known this man for more than a decade. I typically saw him hanging with his friends on the corner across the street from the church. Men gamble, drink, and smoke on this corner all day long. This young man, though, came to me wanting things to change. As we talked, he realized not only did his brother and friends need God, but he needed God. He prayed a prayer of commitment to follow Jesus. He got baptized and became a member of our church. His voracious reading of Scripture astounded me—not just because he read it, but because he altered life to do what it said.

So maybe we all need a few more problems or as James puts it, "trials of many kinds." Jesus told the rich man eternal life would only come by way of problems. It's also what He told His disciples when He said, "Blessed are the poor in spirit, for theirs is the kingdom of heaven" (Matthew 5:3). In those few words we find the power of problems. On the pathway of life, problems whisper in our ear the password to the gate of heaven: "God, I need you."

Andrew Mann is the executive director of Graffiti 2 Community Ministries and pastors Graffiti 2 Baptist Church in South Bronx, New York.

God's Calling Couldn't Fit in My Box

There are different kinds of gifts, but the same Spirit
distributes them. There are different kinds of service,
but the same Lord. There are different kinds of working,
but in all of them and in everyone it is the same God at
work. Now to each one the manifestation of the Spirit
is given for the common good.

—1 Corinthians 12:4–7

What do you want to do once you're done with college?"
a friend asked me during my junior year of high school.
That's always a loaded question. How was I to
pick what I wanted to do for my entire career at sixteen? How is
anyone? But this question had started to feel more weighty over
the preceding few years.

"I think I want to be an editor. I want to use words to serve
Christ," I timidly replied.

This was one of the first times I'd vocalized that to anyone.
I thumbed through one of my textbooks from my Christian
school and realized someone had to edit that. What if that
someone could be me?

I'd always had a penchant for words. I love writing them. I
found joy in correcting other people's grammar. While everyone
else groaned when it came time to diagram a sentence in
English class, I jumped at the opportunity to show my mad
grammar skills off at the board.

Maybe, I thought, this could be my version of ministry—editing for Jesus.

"Save that for the lost people," a teacher who was within earshot chimed in.

My stomach dropped, and I was devastated. But I knew he only had my best interest at heart. He knew I'd surrendered to ministry.

You see, as a thirteen-year-old at my first youth conference, I felt the Lord calling me to ministry. At that point, I was convinced He wanted me in missions. As the years went on, the call to missions became less clear, but the pulling in my heart to "ministry" remained.

And in the world we lived in, ministry couldn't possibly be using words to glorify Jesus. Ministry fit in a box and left me with the options of becoming a pastor's wife, missionary's wife, church secretary, or Christian school teacher. All these things appealed to me, and I would have been honored to be any of the above, but I didn't necessarily feel called to any of them.

I asked for no further clarification, but I continued to ponder in my heart a question similar to this: "Are lost people going to edit writing that builds Christ's kingdom?"

It took a few years, some time spent exploring education, preparing myself for a more traditional ministry role, and some serious conviction from the Holy Spirit, but I realized one day that God really was calling me to use words to glorify Him. I had no idea what that looked like, but I stopped being ashamed of my calling.

I enrolled in a small, Southern Baptist–affiliated university in the middle of nowhere, and I changed my major to English. I was all-in. If God was calling me to this, He'd sustain me in it. That I knew.

"Are you going to be a teacher?" person after person asked.

As an English major, people worry about you. I get it. It's the cliché "this person has no idea what they're going to do with their future, but they obviously like to read" major.

I'd confidently reply, "I'm going to be an editor at a Christian publication."

Usually, I'd get a puzzled stare in return.

The confidence didn't come from me. I knew it sounded crazy. My single mom was a disabled custodian. My mostly absent father was an atheist. I definitely wasn't going to be anyone's draft pick based on my connections. At the time, I had no advantageous mentors in my corner.

The confidence to make such a sweeping statement about my future ministry came because I knew the Savior, and I'd felt His unmistakable leading to use words to build the kingdom.

This confidence came because I'd seen the Lord open doors only He could open and lead, drag, and shove me through.

I sat in a psychology class and listened to a professor mention an interdisciplinary journal in which students could submit research papers. After class, I asked if they needed a volunteer editor. That professor connected me to Dr. Stephen Wilson, the professor who doubled as the journal's editor. After a short conversation, he offered me a job basically on the spot. Again, I was in complete shock. They were going to pay me to edit.

The only explanation for that was God. My resume at the time screamed of inexperience.

The next year I was approached and asked if I wanted to edit the school newsletter. I said yes, enlisted the help of someone who knew what they were doing, and again, set to work doing something that felt really close to the dream God was preparing me for.

A couple years later, Dr. Wilson encouraged me to reach out to Art Toalston, the (now retired) editor of Baptist Press. Dr. Wilson was convinced I should be Baptist Press's summer intern.

In another unmistakable move of God, Art took a chance on me. After a grueling summer of shaping a kid who had no real journalistic experience into a writer, I was hooked on Baptist journalism. I knew that was how God was calling me to use words to glorify Him.

Each of these experiences specifically led me to the next, as did all the other little ones in between.

And now, I spend my days as a senior writer/editor for the International Mission Board. For a living, I get to tell stories that matter. My calling to glorify God through words has manifested in the most overwhelmingly cool way. I talk about the work God is doing among the nations . . . and they pay me.

This isn't just a dream job. It's my dream job. Actually, it's much bigger than I could have dreamed. I'm not being modest when I say, as the Apostle Paul did in 1 Corinthians 15:10, "But by the grace of God I am what I am . . ."

God planted a calling in my heart in 2004. For years, I put God in a box and squeezed this calling right in there with Him, but God is so much bigger than my box. And as Proverbs 19:21 says, "Many are the plans in a person's heart, but it is the LORD's purpose that prevails."

My entire life, but especially my calling, is a testament to God's sovereignty.

Myriah Snyder is the senior writer/editor for the International Mission Board.

Uniquely Created by God

But we have this treasure in jars of clay to show that
this all-surpassing power is from God and not from us.

—2 Corinthians 4:7

When we see someone in need our heart often leaps with compassion to help that person. Sometimes we put too much pressure on ourselves thinking we have the power to bring about change in others' lives. The power of change is delivered by God and in His timing. When a person is ready to change, it is God at work, it is not a person bringing it about. God does work in and through us to help others. Waiting for someone to change is hard, but we should not give up on someone or stop caring. We continue to help and love through truth. Loving in truth means setting healthy boundaries and giving tough love. Sharing the hope of Jesus and helping others discover how they have been uniquely created to serve and worship God encourages people to move past the situations and circumstances they sometimes find themselves in.

We have a pottery ministry at Baptist Friendship House in New Orleans. As our artisans make pottery, it starts with a piece of clay. Utilizing hands or a wheel, the clay is molded into whatever one desires. If the artisan does not like the way the pottery looks, while it is still soft, they can smash it back down and try again. Once the pottery is in the desired shape, it will have to sit on a shelf and dry for a period. The clay, when dry, must be placed in a kiln to fire. After the clay has fired, it is glazed, and put back in the kiln to fire again. The process is time consuming, but once it is finished, you have a strong and beautiful piece of pottery.

Our lives are somewhat like the pottery process. We grow and change over time. Sometimes we are the soft clay and change is slow. The beauty of Jesus is that as long as we have breath, we can start over. His grace, mercy, and forgiveness are available every day. Jesus never gives up on us and we should never give up on others. As we journey with Jesus, we become strong in Him, and He makes something beautiful out of our lives.

I am thankful that, early in my ministry, I had an encounter with a person who taught me the value of waiting on God to work in someone's life. T. J. was in our substance abuse program. He was an alcoholic and had entered our four-month in-house treatment program at Brantley Baptist Center in New Orleans.

As I built a relationship with T. J., I had the opportunity to share Jesus with him. His response was, "God is dog spelled backwards and that is how I feel." T. J. was angry at God and had turned to alcohol to self-medicate his feelings from losing his family in a house fire. I understood he was angry, and I knew God's shoulders were big enough to handle the anger. I must admit, I was just starting out in ministry and to hear someone say God is dog spelled backwards alarmed me. I prayed and tried my best to figure out what to say or do. God placed upon my heart to not judge, but to listen, and continue to care about T. J.

Over time, T. J. came up to me and said, "There may be something to God, would you tell me more about Him?" I shared with T. J., and he asked Jesus to come into his life and forgive him for his sins. I realized in that moment, with time, God melts angry hearts, not me. God molds us and makes us who He wants us to be. T. J. assisted in our shelter registration for people who were experiencing homelessness. He would help register more than two hundred people a day to stay the night at Brantley Baptist Center.

One day T. J. came up to me and said, "Wouldn't it be funny when I die if God fires St. Peter and puts me to registering people in at heaven's gate?"

I said, "My friend, you have come a long way from saying God is dog spelled backwards to wondering what you will do when you get to heaven." His statement was proof to me that only God can change lives. There is no way I could ever change someone's life like that. I am not to judge but to love people and be obedient as God works.

Our experiences make us uniquely who we are. There is no one else in the world like you. Nobody has had your exact experience or your personality. None of us have the same thumbprint. God has taken His time to mold you into the special person you are. The experiences we all have are often not easy and we go through hurt and pain. Satan wants to destroy us, but God desires to use those experiences to help us grow. I often say, God makes good things come out of bad things. T. J.'s tragic experience of losing his family and dealing with alcoholism was horrible, but God uniquely equipped him to reach out to other people with an empathetic ear and with compassion.

As we go through rough times, it is important to realize God is there with us helping us. The joy on the other side of the hurt, pain, and hardship is to gain the perspective that because I have experienced what I have, I am uniquely created to help others. Forgetting not, as we help others, it was God who molded us, not others. We are instruments used by God, but the power is God's. Use the acrostic of POWER to allow God to work through you. **P**ray, **O**ffer ourselves in service to God, **W**orship God, **E**xemplify Jesus, **R**emember God is in control.

Kay Bennett is the executive director of Baptist Friendship House in New Orleans, Louisiana.

Mentors Spark Growth

But the fruit of the Spirit is love, joy, peace, forbearance, kindness, goodness, faithfulness, gentleness and self-control. Against such things there is no law.

—Galatians 5:22–23

The simplicity and purity of the characteristics outlined in Galatians 5 might lead the casual reader to overlook the depth and richness contained in the description of a life truly and completely filled with the Holy Spirit.

A full thirty years now since surrendering my life to Christ, I still struggle to consistently display the full set intact in the purity for which it is intended—at least all pieces at the same time.

Still, the security and confidence I have in being a child of the King provide the environment I need to develop and grow in each of the areas. Most days you'll find a few pieces of fruit shimmering brightly with a genuine desire to point all to Him.

But making my way to showcase all nine characteristics at the same time all the time seems to be a lifelong journey—a journey dependent on the investment of others in me. Reflecting on my half century of life, I can see how God was faithful to place people in my life to help guide me during specific seasons, which assures me He will continue to do the same going forward.

The thread of mentors may not have known who came before or who would follow but each grabbed the baton on cue and stewarded its delivery to the next runner in the relay—all while balancing his or her own life issues.

From parents and extended family who modeled a fierce love, kindness, and goodness to Sunday School teachers, pastors, and other church leaders who faithfully pointed me to the true Author of joy and peace, I have been surrounded and influenced by ripe fruit since birth.

The love and gentleness of a dear friend guided me to the foot of the cross, and the forbearance (patience) of an older mentor instilled the concepts of discipleship and making disciples. Many mentors have taken turns discipling me along the way.

Since those initial days of full surrender followed by a commitment to full-time vocational Christian service, the faithfulness of God and of those He puts in my path continues to fill my soul with awe and adoration.

Whether it be a fellow church member, ministry peer, or dear friend, countless believers ahead of me on the journey have reached back time after time to grab my hand and pull me along.

Sometimes the investment comes in the form of support and encouragement, while other times it sends me to my knees for repentance and recentering.

Many bolster me through praying and reminding me to keep my eyes on Jesus. Others show love and support through their actions and how well they care for me. Still, others offer a listening ear and comforting shoulder during those times the load seems a bit too heavy.

Of course, more times than not, the ninth characteristic of self-control is where I need the most help—and God has been faithful to provide people bold enough to voice concerns along the way.

It's when He drops a carload of those bold voices in my path that I've learned to pay immediate attention—a lesson learned from paying a high price for ignoring them in the past.

How I missed it for so many years, I'm not sure, but I now treasure seeing those dear servants of the Lord step in front of me to get my attention, to slow me from barreling out of control.

What used to frustrate me because I deemed they couldn't possibly understand why I was not taking proper care of myself, now gives me comfort.

The gentle guidance from mentors noting hazards up ahead, pointing out weaknesses I need to address, and challenging me to find a better way keeps me humbly seeking self-control through true self-discipline. Finding the proper rhythms for my day and in my overall faith walk isn't easy with all the pressures and demands that seem to grow extra tentacles each morning, but the effort is possible with those willing to share their secrets and show the way.

As I work to cull the withered parts of my heart to make more room for the Holy Spirit to nurture the fruit planted in me, I am reminded to look around for others who might need to borrow my clippers for a time.

Following the model of those who noticed me and sacrificed to help me grow—and are doing so today and will tomorrow—I am inspired to do the same for others.

The ripple effect makes sense as person after person flourishes from the watering of others and then looks to share the gift rather than hoard it for himself or herself.

The Holy Spirit will surface the who, what, when, where, why, and how at exactly the right time and all we have to do is dive in, knowing we are covered by the grace of our Lord.

As each follower of Jesus Christ showcases genuine love, joy, peace, forbearance (patience), kindness, goodness, faithfulness, gentleness, and self-control, the environment around him or her will no doubt shine brightly with beams from the one true Light.

The hope we have in Christ gives us the courage and strength to not only face each new day, no matter what it brings, but also to seek wisdom and nourishment from the Word in order to nurture our reflection of Him—to genuinely, naturally, and consistently broadcast the fruit of the Spirit.

Jennifer Rash is the president and editor-in-chief for TAB Media Group/The Alabama Baptist, Inc.

Don't Lose Hope

Let us not become weary in doing good, for at the proper time we will reap a harvest if we do not give up.

—Galatians 6:9

A conversation that often comes up in my work with churches is the concern caused by the downward trend of church attendance. If this continues, most agree, some churches will be "out of business" in a certain number of months or even weeks. The trend has a lot to do with both attendance and finances. These two factors show how a church is losing people and how much money is not coming in compared to what is going out. This is a valid and real concern of some of our pastors.

Several years ago, I had a pastor friend, Ron, who had done the analysis on these two factors and that was also his conclusion. If the trend kept going, his church would go "out of business." The trend logically makes sense and is not mathematically incorrect; however, it also does not factor in God's command to persevere regardless.

Over the next several years, what I saw in Ron's ministry was he continued to be faithful and obedient—the church gave away their building for a replant and they made important decisions in regard to their assets so that they could continue blessing kingdom ministries. Ron also began to look for other church employment.

What he did not do, however, was to stop doing outreach in his community during this time. He continued going into the community, not necessarily for the purpose of revitalizing the church, but solely for the purpose of obedience to Christ in carrying out His commands. He was not afraid of what was coming next in ministry, and he also did not stop working.

It has been four years since the trend lines were supposed to take this church down, yet the church still continues to meet every week. Ron is still doing outreach every week. The financial issue in many ways is miraculous. The church continues each year to end in the black. I am convinced that is because Ron has remained faithful to the kingdom work. God's kingdom is still being expanded.

One day, Ron will be able to see the fruit of his labor. A pastor is always interested in his church growing, but Ron began to realize through his experience that this was not what was happening. Rather, he was going to continue being faithful in the work for the sake of the kingdom. He decided he was going to take the command of Jesus in Matthew 6:33 seriously to "seek first the kingdom of God and His righteousness, and all these things will be added unto you" (BSB). For Ron's particular situation, what was going to be "added unto them" was the physical needs that he and the church had.

My story is similar to Ron's story. One evening I came home from my church discouraged after hearing that two more people were leaving the church. This news came after many others had left during the previous six months. The first thing I wanted to do was to find a way out of the situation, yet God clearly showed me that it was not time to give up but time to start praying.

Our church came together and prayed for an extended period of time and we also went to work. We did visitation most Saturdays, did various outreach projects, and knocked on thousands of doors in our neighborhood. We saw God do incredible work in the life of our church that I could never have imagined. We started growing numerically again and began to see many baptisms every year. The church had a renewed spirit of believing God was not through yet and He had a wonderful plan for them. A few months after I left Grace Temple to begin working for the state convention, I witnessed four baptisms of people from different backgrounds. That day I realized the years the church faithfully prayed and worked were now allowing me and others to see a new harvest. What a joy to witness God continuing to do His faithful and good work.

The encouragement of Galatians 6:9 is to not grow weary in doing good because the harvest will eventually come if we do not give up. It is the "doing good" continually that brings about what God has for you. Many American believers get caught up in the lie that nothing should have to take long; therefore, when a church is struggling, things should turn around fast or easy. Ultimately, it takes time to see God do a work sometimes. Author Eugene H. Peterson, borrowing from an atheist philosopher, said following Christ is "a long obedience in the same direction." Long obedience requires someone to not stop, but to continue working to see that it gets done.

Don't lose hope.

I do not know what will happen to every church I have had the privilege of serving. What I do know, however, is that the churches that survive and thrive are the churches that continue to be faithful. Revitalization and replanting are hard work and the churches who accomplish this have one trait in common: they do not give up.

Ryan Jespersen is the executive director of Dallas Baptist Association.

The Power of Prayer

Now to him who is able to do immeasurably more than all we ask or imagine, according to his power that is at work within us.

—Ephesians 3:20

Leaves were falling when I sat down at a table with my pastor and several ministry leaders for a weekly meeting at the church. "We haven't seen any baptisms over the last year, and I'm really burdened about that. Will you pray with me for God to bring people He is saving to our church to be baptized and discipled?"

We each said yes with silent nods, sensing a pastor's heavy heart. Despite a multitude of ministry efforts in the community, the baptismal was dry, and had been for too long.

On that afternoon, our small group had no idea what God was about to do.

Across the ocean, more than ten years before that cool day, Mari* was a teenager in an arid African nation dominated by Islam. Her mother died when she was a child, so her grandmother was raising her and her sister under the controlling eye of their Muslim father. He begrudgingly allowed her to attend a Christian school because it was close to their home. Even though her father did not permit Mari to attend the chapel services, she began hearing her schoolmates sing Christian songs from a distance. She wondered about the happiness heard in their singing. At school, she was given a small Bible, which she read in secrecy. Soon after, Mari surrendered her life to Christ.

Mari's grandmother began to notice how often the young girl retreated to her room. One day she asked her granddaughter what she was doing. "Oh, I'm just reading for school assignments," Mari said. She had not told anyone about becoming a Christian.

Sensing something else was happening, her grandmother removed the door to Mari's room and eventually caught her reading the small Bible. Frightened, Mari looked up at the woman who had been like a mother. She was stunned by what her grandmother said next.

"It's OK. Follow your heart."

The ways of Islam once again surrounded Mari when she was told to wed a Muslim man much older than she. Only a young teenager, she was terrified at the thought of being sent off into a marriage and life she did not choose. But there was nothing she could do.

Despite tearful and frantic pleading, Mari became a child bride and moved to a neighboring African nation with her husband. In the first months, her husband was not home due to his work. When he was there, she managed to find ways to avoid him. Lonely and hopeless, she secretly messaged a friend from her school and asked for help. A devised plan brought Mari back to her home country. But she knew she could not return to her family; she would be forced to go back to the marriage if they found her. Mari was on the run, with nowhere to go.

Like a river forced underground by immovable forces of nature, Mari's life became hidden. Maybe for survival, maybe because of the religious tyranny she was surrounded by. Many years passed before the rest of her story unfolded.

Let's go back to that fall afternoon and the crisp air in the United States. I had taken to heart the prayer request my pastor recently shared. Remembering the promise of Isaiah 65:1, I often prayed that God would reveal Himself to those who did not ask for Him, and that He would be found by those who did not seek Him. I kept a silent vigil, watching and praying with others each week for what God may do.

One Sunday after the closing song ended at church, a friend came to me as I gathered my purse and Bible.

"Laurel*, you've got to meet that lady over there. She came to church last week for the first time and is back this week. She has been telling everyone she wants to be baptized!"

Making my way across the sanctuary toward her, I couldn't help but wonder if this was an answer to our many prayers.

The young lady was already smiling at me as I got to her and introduced myself.

"It's nice to meet you. My name is Mari."

In the following days, I and another friend from church went to Mari's apartment. As we sat with her, Mari shared about her life in Africa—the small Bible, her secret faith in Christ, and the forced marriage. She also shared how she ended up living just a few miles from our church. Most importantly, she clearly sensed God's call to finally make her faith public in baptism.

Mari did just that the next Sunday. Buried with Christ, raised to walk in newness of life.

The baptismal was wet again.

But it wouldn't be the last time the baptistery in the 130-year-old church would be filled with water.

In miraculous, yet simple ways, others soon followed. Young men who came to the United States as children from one country heard the gospel and confessed their faith in the baptistery not long after Mari.

One woman was befriended by Christ-following refugees in her apartment complex and was baptized Christmas Eve.

Another woman walked in the church on the last Sunday of April of the next year. She arrived only in time to hear the announcements at the end of the service.

"If you have surrendered your life to Christ but have never been baptized," the pastor said, "please come talk to me."

The tall woman from East Africa walked up to the front of the room where he was standing. "My name is Alamzah* and I have recently become a Christian. I would like to be baptized, and I need someone to teach me the Bible."

The next week, Alamzah was baptized.

Over a six-month time frame, more than thirty people were baptized, each reminding the church how God moves in the hearts of the unsaved as His people pray.

Laurel Dune is a pseudonym for a lifelong missions advocate.

---

*names changed

May We Always Remember: To Live Is Christ

For to me, to live is Christ and to die is gain.

—Philippians 1:21

Carved on my parents' headstone in a rural church cemetery in southeast Missouri are the profound words of Philippians 1:21: "To live is Christ. To die is gain."

Those eight words sum up Dad's brief fifty-six years on earth as well as Mom's full ninety-four years of life, including nearly four decades anticipating her heavenly reunion with Dad.

On a practical level, what does it mean that our earthly lives represent Christ and death represents gain?

According to Acts 17:28, through Jesus Christ, we as believers "live and move and have our being." That's an all-encompassing description of our daily life in Christ. Wherever we go and whatever we think, feel, say or do, our very being is connected to the presence of Christ.

What about the biblical description of physical death as actual gain? It's all rooted in Christians' eternal life in the presence of Christ. In the words of Jesus in John 14:2–3: "I go to prepare a place for you. And if I go and prepare a place for you, I will come again and receive you to Myself; that where I am, there you may be also" (NKJV). To die in Christ is gain indeed!

I was a mere twenty years old when Dad slipped off to heaven. As a result, I have now spent more than two-thirds of my life with only memories of Dad rather than the daily reality of his presence. Despite the forty-plus years since we last visited together, I still vividly recall many of the life lessons and words of wisdom he shared.

As a Baptist deacon, Sunday School teacher, and lay speaker, Dad often shared biblical insights in a variety of settings. I specifically recall a Wednesday night Bible study he led during my teen years in our home church of First Baptist Church of Portageville, Missouri.

Speaking on the topic of "Three Philosophies of Life," Dad said those three perspectives are:

1. What's mine is mine and you can't have it.
2. What's yours is mine if I can take it.
3. What's mine is yours if you have need of it.

Throughout his life and ministry, I saw Dad consistently choose option number three. Perhaps that's why his outline has stuck with me all these years. He delighted in sharing what he had with others and gently pointing them toward a personal faith walk with Jesus. To live is Christ.

Dad also was a gifted soloist, choir member, and music leader. One of the treasures we received after his memorial service was from a family friend who tracked down a cassette tape of Dad singing a mini-concert during a Sunday morning worship service. Over the years, we have transferred those precious memories to CDs and more recently to digital files.

One of the old hymns he sang that morning was titled "How Beautiful Heaven Must Be." It featured the reassuring refrain, "How beautiful heaven must be, Sweet home of the happy and free; Fair haven of rest for the weary, How beautiful heaven must be." It seemed to be a timely and comforting message from God through Dad to our family: To die is gain.

Some forty years later, I had the bittersweet privilege of speaking at Mom's memorial service in the same familiar setting where our family had gathered for worship so often over the years.

I recall affirming that my mother was "one of the most genuine, dedicated, sincere followers of Jesus I have ever known." I went on to share that Mom didn't just talk her faith, she walked it every day of her life. She trusted God with everything. No matter what came her way, even in the most challenging moments of life, her typical response was, "God will take care of it."

In handwritten memoirs presented to each of her grandchildren, Mom wrote that what she valued most in life was "my relationship with God and seeking to do His will in all things."

Whether raising six kids, teaching Sunday School and Vacation Bible School, serving as associational WMU director, or faithfully ministering to residents at the local nursing home, Mom consistently sought to embody her favorite Scripture verse, "I can do all things through Christ who strengthens me" (Philippians 4:13 NKJV).

Obviously, many of you reading these words may have grown up in a home with dedicated Christian parents as well. Even for those who grew up amid far more difficult family dynamics, you have the opportunity to break that cycle in your own life and family. So what's the story of hope from a kind, loving couple who lived their lives in faithful dedication to Christ?

For those of us who had the privilege of being nurtured in a strong family of faith, there's the lasting hope we gained through the meaningful life lessons we learned from their examples. For those of us who are parents and grandparents, we have the hope that we also will live as mentors, role models, and encouragers for the generations who follow.

I'm not speaking here of the worldly hope of "Gosh, I hope that comes true." Rather, I'm pointing to the confident hope that we as believers have based on God's assurance that "all things work together for good to them that love God" (Romans 8:28 KJV).

Always remember those timeless words of wisdom etched on a headstone and inscribed on believers' hearts across the ages: To live is Christ. To die is gain. May we joyfully embrace those truths every day of our earthly journey.

Trennis Henderson, a longtime Christian journalist, is a former WMU national correspondent and currently serves as regional correspondent for TAB Media and The Baptist Paper.

Unexpected Visitor

Here I am! I stand at the door and knock. If anyone
hears my voice and opens the door, I will come in and
eat with that person, and they with me.

—Revelation 3:20

When a visitor arrives at one's home, he or she usually
arrives at the front door, right? Imagine my surprise
while home alone one day after school, when I heard
an unexpected knock at the back door. Our back door was solid
glass and so I could clearly see who was standing there—my
grandfather.

While this may sound odd, it was actually normal. My grandfather was notorious for showing up at our house without notice. Although he lived two hours away, at that point in time, my
family lived the closest we'd ever lived to him and so I think a
two-hour trek across the East Tennessee mountains was an easy
trip compared to other places we'd lived prior to that time (one
of those being overseas as missionaries).

When my grandfather was asked why he came to our house
without letting us know, he said, "Aw, I just took a notion and
figured I'd stop by!"

And while we sometimes had to change our schedules
and routine to accommodate our unexpected visitor, those
rearrangements would turn into some of the most joyful,
heartwarming times of hearing stories of his life experiences or
my dad's childhood, looking through old photos, and gathering

around the table to enjoy his favorite dessert—yellow cake with chocolate icing.

How I would give anything today if there was a knock at my door and I opened it to find my grandfather. I would gladly welcome him into my home and share with him what all God is doing in my life. But he has since passed on to heaven—the place he talked about going for as long as I can remember.

In Revelation 3:20, Jesus reminds us that He stands at our door and knocks. While this isn't a literal door, rather the door of our hearts, He still shows up unexpected and awaits an invitation to be welcomed inside. This is true for the suffering sinner, but it's also true for the hopeless believer.

Jesus makes sure we won't miss Him because His presence at the door isn't silent. How do we know? Two ways. The first is the use of the word "knock." Knocking is not a quiet action, it requires striking something noisily to demand attention—think exuberant salesperson or giddy trick-or-treaters. Why do these individuals knock on the door of your home? Because they want you to open the door to share in their excitement.

The second way Jesus makes sure we won't miss Him is because He says we will hear His voice at the door. Have you ever called a parent or friend on the phone just to hear their voice? We do that sometimes because hearing a familiar, loving voice is soothing and comforting. If we feel that way about a person we love, can you imagine how it will feel to hear the voice of Jesus, the ultimate Comforter, the most Wonderful Counselor, and the mighty Prince of Peace?

Now in terms of this verse, Jesus' voice and knocking may or may not be audible. Jesus may speak to your heart when you come across a verse while reading Scripture during your daily quiet time. You may hear Him knocking on your heart as you listen to a sermon or Bible lesson and walk away stirred. It's even possible for Jesus to use friends, family members, or even strangers to speak the truths of His presence into your heart.

And yet, despite the fact that Jesus is at the door, making all sorts of commotion to let us know He is there, the responsibility of welcoming in that peace and comfort and love rests on us. It is our choice to listen to the knocking and to His voice and it is also our choice to open the door and say, "Come on in!" Like any loving Father, God hopes we choose to receive life in and with Him by believing in His Son, Jesus, so that we can be fully and completely His. "Yet to all who did receive him, to those who believed in his name, he gave the right to become children of God" (John 1:12).

But, oh, the joy of welcoming in our Savior when we make the choice to do so. The end of Revelation 3:20 talks about sharing a meal with Jesus. Is the focus here on the food, though? No. The focus here is that welcoming Jesus into the door of our hearts means we will be in community with Him. It means our relationship with Him will be deeper and richer and beyond our wildest dreams. In the New Testament, we see that Jesus dines with those closest to Him—His disciples and His followers.

In those times of sharing food, Jesus' close friends glean profound insights into Jesus and His purpose and plan. The same is true for us. When we open the door and invite Jesus fully in, partaking of and savoring the spiritual food of His words and deeds, He will reveal His purpose and plan for us in many different ways, at many different times, and that involve incomprehensible opportunities.

It can seem a little frightening when there is an unexpected knock at a door. However, the lost and disheartened need not fear the surprising visitor who shows up in Revelation 3:20; rather, they should be filled with hope. Hope that a comforting friend is standing on the other side (John 15:14). Hope that once we let Him in, He will never leave or forsake us (Deuteronomy 31:6; Hebrews 13:5). Hope that His revelations will be for our good and not our disaster (Jeremiah 29:11). Hope that in His presence will be joy and blessings forever (Psalm 16:11).

Allison Young is the publication and project coordinator for the Southern Baptist Convention Executive Committee.

Restoration Through Adoption

The LORD is my shepherd, I lack nothing. He makes me
lie down in green pastures, he leads me beside quiet
waters, he refreshes my soul. He guides me along the
right paths for his name's sake.

—Psalm 23:1–3

Arkansas Baptist Children's Homes and Family Ministries (ABCH) has a mission to build, strengthen, and restore Arkansas families for God's glory. Every child deserves to be connected to loving, nurturing relationships. Through Connected Foster Care, ABCH pursues reunification with the biological family until it is not an option. When reunification is no longer an option, the goal is adoption.

"He makes me lie down in green pastures. He leads me beside quiet waters."

Arkansas Baptist Ranch accepted a sibling group of seven into care. The children had been in foster care for a while but were not living together in the same home as brothers and sisters. Keeping brothers and sisters together provides children a sense of belonging and safety. Thankfully, when they came to live at the Ranch, they were once again able to live as siblings in the same home. This was the first step of reunification for the children. Unfortunately for these children, their parents' rights had been terminated.

Meanwhile, Jeff and Cassie Lothe and their two sons were approved to open their home for adoption through the Arkansas Division of Children and Family Services (DCFS). The first and only time the Lothes were ever contacted was about this sibling group of seven. The Lothes gladly agreed to begin the process.

Cassie said, "My initial thought was there's no way. We don't have a vehicle big enough. We'll have to build some beds, lots of bunk beds, get dressers for everyone, and get mattresses donated from friends and family." The Lothes frequently made weekend trips from their home to the Ranch, and that allowed the Lothes to meet the children in a location familiar to them.

Once the Lothe family was paired with them, something wonderful began to happen—the kids felt as if they were in a family once again. One story Cassie shared was about the four-year-old in the sibling group, Shiloh. After staying with them one weekend, she did not want to get out of the car when they returned to the Ranch and repeatedly told her Ranch caregivers, "I don't have to listen to you, 'cause I have a new mom now." Within a few months, it was official. The Lothes decided to adopt this sibling group.

The preadoptive stage was about six months long. During this time the children lived in the Lothes' home. Ranch staff continued to offer them supportive care throughout this process. They walked the family through how to care for a group of nine siblings (counting their two birth children). This included preparing menus, cooking large meals, organizing the home, budgeting, grocery shopping, and so much more.

Ranch staff called and checked on them often, advocating for this family, even when they faced challenges. The Lothes did not want to give up on this sibling group, and the Ranch staff saw their love for these children. They continued supporting them.

"Without that advocacy, the kids may not have been adopted," says Brandy Urioste, director of Arkansas Baptist Ranch.

Even after the adoption was final, the Ranch still supported them. They were there to encourage them, help them face daily life issues, and answer every phone call. The Ranch will continue to be there for them. A lasting bond has been formed.

Their church was also a significant advocate for them. The Lothes were blessed by a family who acted as if they were blood relatives, helping them with everything they needed—advice (specifically when dealing with preteens), cooking, and organizing.

The Lothes acknowledged there were difficult and questioning times while adjusting to this large sibling group, but the blessings always seemed to outweigh the concerns.

"There were times we doubted our calling," Cassie shared. "We felt we weren't equipped or suited for the overwhelming needs of these kids. They have been with us for three years now, and what has been so rewarding is seeing our kids come to know Christ. They are wanting to attend youth group, sing worship songs at the top of their lungs, and they are really trying hard to do the right things. When I see them loving the Lord like that, it reminds me that Christ loves us so much more. These babies just needed a pathway to find Him, and we are so humbled He chose us to help them on that journey."

"He refreshes my soul. He guides me along the right paths for his name's sake."

What a great example of God's perfect timing. The Lothes had become an adoptive family at the exact time this sibling group of seven needed a family they could call their own, a forever home. The Ranch support provided a way for adoption to happen. Without that support, this family of four may not have become a family of eleven. Their family is now complete, the seven siblings are restored to a new family, and they are following in the paths of righteousness for His name's sake together. God had a hand in this adoption from the beginning, and He used the Ranch to intercede for them. This family's story shows a wonderful picture of who Christ is to us and how He restores hope and restores families.

We can have hope because Christ is our ultimate source of hope. Without His intercession for us, there would be no hope; but because He chose us, we can choose Him. Just as this sibling group needed a forever home, so do we. That home is with Christ and the hope He gives.

Charles Flynn is the director of operations for Arkansas Baptist Children's Homes and Family Ministries.

Cloud of Witnesses

Therefore, since we are surrounded by such a great
cloud of witnesses, let us throw off everything that
hinders and the sin that so easily entangles. And let
us run with perseverance the race marked out for us,
fixing our eyes on Jesus, the pioneer and perfecter of
faith. For the joy set before him he endured the cross,
scorning its shame, and sat down at the right hand of
the throne of God.

—Hebrews 12:1–2

Nursing is considered a most noble profession and I am
honored to be a part of that profession. At a very early
age, literally at the feet of my WMU-loving grandmother
(think early pedicures), I started to sense God's calling to become
a nurse. I began to walk in that direction and God opened door
after door for my calling to become a reality. I can still hear my
grandmother's voice saying, "You would be a wonderful nurse."
My hope in Christ and His calling on my life sustained me and
moved me forward.

As a young mother and nurse serving on the mission
field, I was challenged to find how nursing would fit into our
ministry. Again, my hope in Christ opened doors for me to begin
teaching nursing at the local Red Cross office. Through those
connections, a Christian nurse fellowship was begun at the local
hospital. What a joy it was to hear nurses say to me, "We *need*
this time of Bible study and prayer together. It helps us face the
challenges we see in the hospital and at home."

As our family transitioned back to life in the United States from Chile, my hope in Christ guided me to begin hospice nursing. What a privilege it is to hold the hands of those leaving this earth and the hands of those who are left behind. Repeatedly I saw how those who have hope in Christ experienced a peace that passes all understanding. This was true for those as they breathed their last breath and for those who continued breathing through the pain of loss and grief. I have heard so many families and loved ones say to me, "I don't know how someone deals with death if they do not have hope in Jesus Christ."

Hope in Christ led me to nursing education. Nursing students are the hope for the future of our nursing profession. Their strong educational foundation is critical, but their spiritual foundation is eternal. Taking nursing students on international medical mission trips has been a source that has strengthened that foundation. So many students have said to me, "This experience has changed my life."

Throughout my life, my hope in Christ has guided me through many chapters. In early March 2020, I was returning from a medical mission trip to Mully Children's Family in Ndalani, Kenya. As we worked that week with more than five thousand patients, we became aware of the rising concerns of COVID in the United States and around the world. Our hope in Christ gave us the assurance we were exactly where God wanted us to be. We arrived back in the US on March 15, 2020, the last day the JFK airport would be open to international arrivals for months. God's timing is always perfect.

The COVID-19 global pandemic has been challenging in many ways. Nurses have experienced high patient censuses of critical care patients, symptoms that are difficult to treat, new protocols that are ever-changing, and suffering that seems to never end. Carole Bailey, critical care nurse manager in South Carolina says, "I remember specifically the call I received that morning when we had admitted our first COVID-19 patient. I cried hard and ugly. I wept before the Lord, fearful of the many unknowns associated with COVID-19. I questioned God if I was experienced enough to care for these patients who had been diagnosed with this virus. My husband held me and prayed with me and for me and our team. During this moment, God spoke to me, saying that He had never promised it would be easy. You can do this. Life, work, relationships, and daily tasks are hard these days. But we must remember as Christian nurses that we are made to take care of these patients and their families and persevere during the hard times." I've heard from so many other nurses and healthcare professionals who repeat their hope in Christ is what has sustained them during these types of challenges.

Carole goes on to say, "As Christian nurses, we are facing many challenges. Our team of critical care nursing staff have witnessed too many deaths over these last twenty months, more than I have ever seen in my lifetime as a nurse. COVID-19 has not only had a major impact on our frontline workers but especially our patients and their families and their loved ones.

"Sometimes, we are the only physical person with the patient as they breathe their last breath. We are praying with them and for them and we are singing hymns to them and touching and holding their hand in their fleeting moments on earth. The most disheartening challenge of all is when you know your patient is a nonbeliever in Christ, lost and actively dying. Our words and presence are often the last witness these dying patients will hear or experience. We can pray for them, and we can stay with them as they transition into eternity. For a Christian nurse when the patient death of a lost person occurs, it is a very deep hurt and extreme loss. We want to do all we can to help sustain and save a life both physically and especially spiritually. Hope in Christ overcomes fear every time."

As the verses in Hebrews remind us, there many who have gone before us who are cheering us on. There are voices we continue to hear, reminding us of our hope in Christ as we "fix our eyes on Jesus." We know that as nurses we stand on the shoulders of so many other Christian nurses who have blazed the way for us and have given us a beautiful legacy. Baptist Nursing Fellowship (BNF), an organization I have been a member of for many years, is part of the legacy we have as Christian nurses. BNF offers nurses the opportunity to empower, educate, and encourage nurses to fulfill Christ's mission through healing skills. "For such a time as this," BNF offers a space of renewal of our hope in Christ so that we can touch the hands of those in difficult and dark places. Christian nurses join Carole's voice in saying, "Hope in Christ overcomes fear every time."

Marilyn Graves is the executive director of Baptist Nursing Fellowship.

Forever, for All Peoples

Then I looked and heard the voice of many angels,
numbering thousands upon thousands, and ten
thousand times ten thousand. They encircled the
throne and the living creatures and the elders. In a
loud voice they were saying:
"Worthy is the Lamb, who was slain,
to receive power and wealth and wisdom and strength
and honor and glory and praise!"
Then I heard every creature in heaven and on earth
and under the earth and on the sea, and all that is in
them, saying:
"To him who sits on the throne and to the Lamb
be praise and honor and glory and power,
for ever and ever!"
—Revelation 5:11–13

Near the end of his life, the Apostle John had every reason to be discouraged. After a lifetime of faithful and fruitful ministry, John found himself alone. All of his fellow disciples had been martyred, and John found himself exiled on the island of Patmos as a result of Roman persecution.

Yet against this backdrop, in a moment when circumstances appeared bleak and things seemed uncertain, John was given a vision from the Lord that pointed to a future of rejoicing. John's vision is recorded for us in Revelation 5, and it gives us a foretaste of the future. That vision includes a picture of thousands and thousands of people from every tribe and language and people and nation worshipping Jesus. In verse 12, they shout in a loud voice, "Worthy is the Lamb, who was slain!"

The breathtaking vision God gave John was not just him in his day, but it is also for us in our day. This vision is a picture of what everyone who has trusted Jesus will experience one day. It's a vision of what forever will be like for all peoples who trust Christ.

Five themes that emerge from the passage should guide us as we seek to be witnesses for Jesus who work together to reach the lost in our own neighborhood, city, state, nation, and world.

We should be people of prayer.

Revelation 5:8 describes golden bowls of incense, which Scripture says symbolize the prayers of the saints, a sweet aroma to God. This verse gives us comfort and confidence that God not only hears our prayers, but He also delights in them. If we are going to reach those without Christ, prayer cannot be our last resort. Prayer must be our first priority.

We should expect suffering.

In verse 9, the saints sing, "You were slain, And have redeemed us to God by Your blood" (NKJV). God saves sinners through the suffering of His Son. Scripture is clear that without the shedding of blood there is no forgiveness of sin. Believers throughout the centuries have suffered for the name of Jesus. Suffering can take many forms. It could mean greater persecution, but it could also mean making difficult changes in our churches and how we do ministry. We must be willing to set aside our preferences, programs, and the past to ask, "What can we do to reach a changing world for Jesus?"

We must remember that salvation is in Christ alone.

Those worshipping in Revelation 5 were redeemed by the blood of Christ. Acts 4:12 summarizes the truth underscored throughout Scripture—there is no other name by which people can be saved. All saving faith is focused on and found in the Son of God, yet there are billions of people alive today who have never heard the name of Christ. We must be about the business of bringing Jesus to people who have not heard and keeping Jesus at the center of all we do.

We must remember that the gospel is for all peoples.

Who belongs to the multitude that John describes in this passage? All peoples. Note, it's not all people, but all peoples. We will never know God's glory until we understand that His glory is for all nations. God is multiethnic, multilinguistic, and multinational. He sent His Son to die for people of all nations and all tribes. The awful sin of racism that plagues our nation and our world isn't a political issue or a social issue. It is a gospel issue. The church must be the primary force in solving this issue as we point people to Christ.

We must prioritize worship.

Ultimately, Revelation 5 is all about worship. In this passage, we see thousands from the nations worshipping Jesus. Worship isn't just a time we set aside on Sundays. Our entire lives should be expressions of worship to our Lord and Savior. God desires more worshippers, and the church is God's "plan A" for reaching a lost world.

If we want to be a church that reaches all peoples to worship, we must be ready to stand on God's Word and the exclusivity of salvation in Jesus Christ. We must be ready and willing to change and to suffer as we proclaim the name of Jesus. First and foremost, we must be fueled by prayer. These five things should unite us as a gospel people.

We don't know when this picture of what the Apostle John recorded will come to pass. We don't know when the day will come when we will all be around the throne in worship. But what we do know is this: if we believe this is true about tomorrow, it changes everything about how we should live for today.

Todd Unzicker is the executive director-treasurer of the Baptist State Convention of North Carolina.

Racial Unity Is Central to the Gospel of Jesus Christ

> Here there is no Gentile or Jew, circumcised or
> uncircumcised, barbarian, Scythian, slave or free, but
> Christ is all, and is in all. Therefore, as God's chosen
> people, holy and dearly loved, clothe yourselves
> with compassion, kindness, humility, gentleness and
> patience. Bear with each other and forgive one another
> if any of you has a grievance against someone. Forgive
> as the Lord forgave you. And over all these virtues put
> on love, which binds them all together in perfect unity.
>
> —Colossians 3:11–14

History always seems to repeat itself. Sad, but true. In almost every generation there has been repeated and ongoing instances of racial tension. Issues along the line of race and ethnicity have always been present in culture, dating back to the beginning of time. Why is that the case? I daresay it's because all humans are fallen, broken, and sinful people and are in desperate need of salvation.

As an African American woman, I have experienced racism throughout my adult life, and sadly, the majority of my experiences have happened in churches. I have been told that Black people are cursed because of the curse of Ham in the Bible.

This is erroneous teaching regarding the passage of Scripture found in Genesis 9 and unfortunately, this lie has been taught in churches for generations.

I have had people use racial epithets and slurs toward me, treat me indifferently, undermine, devalue, disrespect me, and make disparaging comments toward me because of the color of my skin. These memories and experiences of how I have repeatedly been treated were painful then and they are still painful today. However, I do have hope because God has allowed me to be in wonderful relationships with Christians of all ethnicities who have demonstrated kindness, grace, love, and compassion toward me. I am deeply thankful for and encouraged by these relationships and friendships.

As Christians, why should we talk about racial unity?

Racial Unity Is Important to God

God grieves over the sin of racism and it breaks His heart because all men are made in His image and in His likeness. Genesis 1:27 says, "So God created mankind in his own image, in the image of God he created them, male and female he created them." Scripture is clear on this subject and passages on race and ethnicity are woven throughout the Bible.

The Apostle John says in Revelation 7:9–10, "After this I looked, and there before me was a great multitude that no one could count, from every nation, tribe, people and language, standing before the throne and in front of the Lamb. They were wearing white robes and were holding palm branches in their hands. And they cried out in a loud voice: 'Salvation belongs to our God, who sits on the throne, and to the Lamb.'" God's desire is that people from every tongue, tribe, and nation will stand before His throne and worship Him for eternity. God loves every single person whom He created in His image, and unity across racial lines is important to Him.

Racial Unity Is Vital to the Message of the Church

The Bible paints a clear picture of the unity important to Christ. In Jesus' prayer for all believers in John 17:20–21, He said, "My prayer is not for them alone. I pray also for those who will believe in me through their message, that all of them may be one, Father, just as you are in me and I am in you. May they also be in us so that the world may believe that you have sent me." Racial unity must be a priority in the church and in the life of every follower of Jesus Christ. We, the church, are to be living testaments of the love, grace, mercy, and forgiveness of God. The world will know this message of unity is true by the love we have for one another.

Racial Unity Is Critical to the Message of the Gospel

The walls of division we see in culture today are walls made by humans, not by God. Oftentimes, we are the ones who create the barriers that divide us from each other. Jesus' last charge to the church in Mathew 28:19–20 was, "Therefore go and make disciples of all nations, baptizing them in the name of the Father and of the Son and of the Holy Spirit, and teaching them to obey everything I have commanded you." Division around race and ethnicity is contrary to the gospel and, as Christians, we must not be silent about it. Christ died to make us one in Him. Ephesians 2:14–15 says, "For he himself is our peace, who has made the two groups one and has destroyed the barrier, the dividing wall of hostility, by setting aside in his flesh the law with its commands and regulations." God's plan and purpose through Christ was to create unity among believers so the gospel could be proclaimed to all people.

It is critical we elevate our kingdom identity as Christians and followers of Christ rather than elevating our racial identity over those who don't look like us because all people are made in God's image. The gospel was meant to transcend issues along the lines of race because, ultimately, the gospel was meant to unify people. Jesus Christ is our only example of someone who loved all people perfectly. His life is the standard we are to follow and my hope is that this message on racial unity will help us all remember that God's love shatters all barriers because of the finished work of Christ on the cross.

Adrianna Anderson is the women's ministry associate at Hunter Street Baptist Church in Hoover, Alabama.

Song of Hope

Sing to the LORD a new song; sing to the LORD, all the earth. Sing to the LORD, praise his name; proclaim his salvation day after day. Declare his glory among the nations, his marvelous deeds among all peoples.

—Psalm 96:1–3

As the daughter of a pastor who taught from time to time but mostly led worship, I've grown up in church all of my life. Singing has been part of my life for as long as I can remember. The definition for sing is to make musical sound with the voice. The definition for praise is to give verbal or expressive admiration. My dad taught me from a young age to sing to the Lord and praise His name.

"Sing to the LORD a new song; sing to the LORD, all the earth."

This lesson has served me well in some very hard times in my life. When death comes to your family, your hope can feel far away. This happened to my family this last year. My dad had a stroke when I was in college, but his health had not diminished considerably until the last few years. He had another stroke right before I got engaged. This time his speech, his ability to swallow, and mostly any movement he had left was affected.

"Sing to the LORD, praise his name; proclaim his salvation day after day."

My family has strong faith, for which I am thankful, and it is what gave us hope that he would be healed and recover. However, on April 27, 2021, our heavenly Father took my earthly dad home. You see, his hope was made sight on that day as he came face to face with the God of heaven. We know this because of our hope in Christ.

"Declare his glory among the nations, his marvelous deeds among all peoples."

Even in the midst of the trials my dad went through with his health the last few years, leading up to him transitioning from this life to the next, we would lean into the songs he loved to sing to the Lord. He loved the choruses from the 1990s and Black gospel singers. He loved songs like "My Tribute" by Andraé Crouch. His favorite hymn was "Blessed Assurance." I think the reason for his love of these songs is because they point our hearts to praise the Lord. They point to the salvation we can find in Christ alone. They point to hope.

This hope my dad had and that I have is a hope that does not disappoint. It's a tangible hope. It's a hope you can hold on to when everything else goes away. You can have a song in your heart when hard things happen. It's this hope that allowed me to sing songs following his transitioning in church and at his funeral. When I miss my dad, the Father always brings these songs of hope to mind and my heart finds comfort there.

May God put a new song of hope in your heart. May you continue to sing a praise song of worship to Him even during difficult times as you find your hope in Him.

April Ott is a senior student mobilization associate at the International Mission Board.

God's Story of Hope

"For I know the plans I have for you," declares the LORD,
"plans to prosper you and not to harm you, plans to
give you hope and a future."

—Jeremiah 29:11

Matt and Marty had a biological son and also adopted a daughter with severe medical needs. Marty had just turned forty and figured they had enough to handle without adding a baby to the mix, until she heard his story. The baby's birth mother is from China. She took a research job at a university in the US to have a child since Chinese law prohibited her from having another child in her country. The birth father is a lawyer and stayed in China.

The birth mother only speaks Chinese. The birth mother fell at thirty-six weeks and had a placental abruption. Medical records report the baby had to be resuscitated ten times.

The Chinese pastor and his wife, who had been ministering to the woman, were present at the hospital and translated. When the birth mom asked what was wrong with the baby, the pastor's wife said, "I don't know. We just need to pray." As they finished praying, the baby started moving his little pinky finger.

Medical personnel suggested all life-sustaining measures be removed except for comfort. Because of the severity of the incident at birth, they said the child would never be able to walk, talk, or breathe on his own. They told the birth mother the baby would die, and she needed to just let him go.

The birth mother said, "I can't. A man appeared to me in a dream last night and said my son would live. I don't know who it was."

Of course, the pastor's wife knew who it was and shared the gospel with her. During her time in the hospital, the birth mother accepted Christ.

She wanted to choose a biblical name for her baby boy. The birth mother chose the name Noah because God used Noah to save the lives of his family. A doctor determined the baby should be flown to Birmingham, Alabama, and undergo dialysis. The pastor's wife called the birth father to update him and suggested he pray to Jesus. The birth father got so angry he hung up on her just as the helicopter was coming to pick up Noah and take him to Birmingham.

A few weeks later, the birth father called and said a man appeared to him in a dream and told him to ask the pastor's wife about this Christian Jesus. So she shared the gospel with him, and he accepted Christ.

About three months later, the birth father came to the US to make a plan to get Noah home. At that time, he and his wife were both baptized. Noah would be refused medical care in China. And the birth parents' absence was putting their other son in jeopardy. They made the difficult decision to put Noah up for adoption with a Christian agency in the US.

The infant began dialysis at a hospital in Birmingham, Alabama. That's where Matt and Marty were introduced to Noah's story. Matt and Marty knew all about dialysis because their adopted daughter, Daisy, was on hemodialysis. This is a procedure by which a machine and a special filter act as an artificial kidney to clean the blood. Daisy was reported to be the youngest person in the world to be given this particular treatment. You must be thirty-five kilos (about seventy-seven pounds) to qualify. She weighed exactly thirty-five kilos when the procedure started.

Matt and Marty were approached about adopting Noah. They slipped away for a meal to discuss the situation. They already had one child getting dialysis treatment. Could God really ask them to take on another?

How would the other children respond? Matt and Marty were Daisy's first permanent family since entering foster care at age three. How would she handle the displacement? They approached the subject one night at the dinner table.

Matt asked, "How would you feel about getting a baby?"

Their son asked, "A baby what?"

Matt said, "A baby human." He explained Noah's medical needs included a feeding tube at the time.

Matt and Marty held their breath waiting for ten-year-old Daisy's response. She stood up from the table and raised her hands and shouted, "Thank You, Jesus, for giving us someone like me!" They all went to the hospital the next day.

Noah's medical condition didn't scare his new family members because they were used to wires and tubes. Noah has had countless people coming and going from his room since birth. His tiny body must have sensed something different. When his forever family arrived to meet him, he fell asleep within thirty seconds. Everyone in the room began weeping. Medical professionals hadn't ever seen him comfortable with anyone. When it came time for the adoption, even the doctors and nurses at the hospital took up an offering to help cover expenses.

Matt and Marty began doing two forms of dialysis in their home. Daisy was getting hemodialysis. Noah was receiving peritoneal dialysis. A doctor once joked if they added another child on dialysis, they could become a dialysis center.

While it was never easy, the family did grow into a rhythm. They were within twenty minutes of Children's of Alabama in Birmingham, where medical staff had treated both Daisy and Noah since birth. At this point Daisy had already received one kidney transplant. Unfortunately, her tiny body rejected the first kidney. Noah was on a list to receive a kidney. It seemed their best option was Birmingham. Then God called Matt and Marty to leave the South. What would they do?

God nudged Matt's heart about the needs in Idaho. Marty's response: "You know it touches Canada, and it is very cold?" They would be three hours away from the children's hospital in Salt Lake. Was this really the best? Even medical professionals at the Birmingham children's hospital did not respond favorably when they heard the news of a potential move. They had cared for these children since birth and wanted the very best for them. Daisy, an African American child, would have a better chance of a kidney donor in Alabama where the African American population is nearly 30 percent, compared to less than 1 percent in Idaho. They were told if she made it to eighteen without receiving a transplant, she would transfer to the adult list and would most likely pass away while waiting for a kidney donor. How did this move possibly make sense? The answer is God's economy.

In 2014, right before the family moved, Noah received his transplant. That required Marty and Noah to stay in Birmingham until he could travel. Matt and the other two children moved to Idaho. Six months after Marty and Noah joined the rest of the family, a call came from a hospital in Idaho. There was a live donor match for Daisy, and she received her second transplant in 2015 when she was fourteen, thanks to a program that was not offered in Alabama. Only God could orchestrate events like these.

It's been a constant whirlwind for Matt and Marty. They fostered three more children whose father got off drugs and sobered up. He accepted Christ, along with his children. The father and oldest daughter were baptized. Matt and Marty's children get to see redemption and how God can work in the midst of seemingly impossible situations.

Now Marty is a foster parent trainer for her area in Idaho. At the close of the training sessions, the father of the children Matt and Marty fostered gives testimony of Christ's work in his life and the support of the church in the reunification of his family.

Marty says, "We're glad to share our story. It's God's story." Yes, it is, with Jesus as the centerpiece. There is indeed hope in Christ.

God always involves us in His plans. Are you living out His purposes for your life?

Sandy Wisdom-Martin serves as the executive director-treasurer for national WMU.

How to Become a Christian

We hope you have enjoyed reading *Because of Hope: Reflections of Faith*. You're not here by accident. God loves you. He wants you to have a personal relationship with Him through Jesus, His Son. Only one thing separates you from God—sin.

The Bible describes sin in many ways. Most simply, sin is our failure to measure up to God's holiness and His righteous standards. We sin by things we do, choices we make, attitudes we show, and thoughts we entertain. We also sin when we fail to do right things. The Bible affirms our own experience: "there is none righteous, not even one" (see Ecclesiastes 7:20). No matter how good we try to be, none of us do right things all the time.

People tend to divide themselves into groups of good people and bad people. But God says every person who has ever lived is a sinner, and any sin separates us from God. No matter how we might classify ourselves, this includes you and me. We are all sinners.

> For all have sinned and fall short of the glory of God.
> (Romans 3:23)

Many people are confused about the way to God. Some think they will be punished or rewarded according to how good they are. Some think they should make things right in their lives before they try to come to God. Others find it hard to understand how God could love them when other people don't seem to.

I have great news for you. God *does* love you. He loves you more than you can ever imagine. And there's nothing you can do to make Him stop. Yes, our sins demand punishment—the punishment of death and separation from God. But because of His great love, God sent His only Son Jesus to die for our sins.

God demonstrates his own love for us in this: While we were still sinners, Christ died for us. (Romans 5:8)

For you to come to God you must get rid of your sin problem. But in our own strength, not one of us can do this. You can't make yourself right with God by being a better person. Only God can rescue us from our sins. He is willing to do this not because of anything you can offer Him, but just because He loves you.

He saved us, not because of righteous things we had done, but because of his mercy. (Titus 3:5)

God's grace allows you to come to Him, not your efforts to "clean up your life" or work your way to heaven. You can't earn it. It's a free gift.

For it is by grace you have been saved, through faith— and this is not from yourselves, it is the gift of God— not by works, so that no one can boast. (Ephesians 2:8–9)

For you to come to God, the penalty of your sin must be paid. God's gift to you is His Son, Jesus, who paid the debt for you when He died on the cross.

For the wages of sin is death, but the gift of God is eternal life in Christ Jesus our Lord. (Romans 6:23)

Jesus paid the price for your sin, and mine, by giving His life on a cross at a place called Calvary, just outside of the city walls of Jerusalem in ancient Israel. God brought Jesus back from the dead. God provided the way for you to have a personal relationship with Him through Jesus. When we realize how deeply our sin grieves the heart of God and how desperately we need a Savior, we are ready to receive God's offer of salvation.

To admit we are sinners means turning away from our sin and selfishness and turning to follow Jesus. The biblical word for this is *repentance*. Repentance means we change our thinking about how grievous sin is, so our thinking is in line with God's.

All that's left for you to do is accept the gift that Jesus is holding out for you right now.

> If you declare with your mouth, "Jesus is Lord," and
> believe in your heart that God raised him from the
> dead, you will be saved. For it is with your heart that
> you believe and are justified, and it is with your mouth
> that you profess your faith and are saved.
> (Romans 10:9–10)

God says if you believe in His Son Jesus, you can live forever with Him in glory.

> For God so loved the world that he gave his one and
> only Son, that whoever believes in him shall not perish
> but have eternal life. (John 3:16)

Are you ready to accept the gift of eternal life that Jesus is offering right now? Let's review what this commitment involves:

I acknowledge I'm a sinner in need of a Savior—this is to repent or turn away from sin.

I believe in my heart that God raised Jesus from the dead—this is to trust that Jesus paid the full penalty for my sins.

I confess Jesus is my Lord and my God—this is to surrender control of my life to Jesus.

I received Jesus as my Savior forever—this is to accept that God has done for me and in me what He promised.

If it is your sincere desire to receive Jesus into your heart as your personal Lord and Savior, then talk to God from your heart. Here's a suggested prayer:

Lord Jesus, I know that I'm a sinner and I do not deserve eternal life. But I believe You died and rose from the grave to make me a new creation and to prepare me to dwell in Your presence forever. Jesus, come into my life, take control of my life, forgive my sins, and save me. I am now placing my trust in You alone for my salvation, and I accept Your free gift of eternal life. Amen.

If you trusted in Jesus as your Lord and Savior, please let us know. We want to rejoice in what God has done in your life and help you to grow spiritually.

If you have questions or concerns you would like help with, please call or write to let us know. We're here to help you understand the love that Jesus is offering you for free, no matter who or where you are. Email us at email@wmu.org, call 1-800-968-7301, or write to us at: Woman's Missionary Union, 100 Missionary Ridge, Birmingham, Alabama 35242.